GEOMETRY & ART

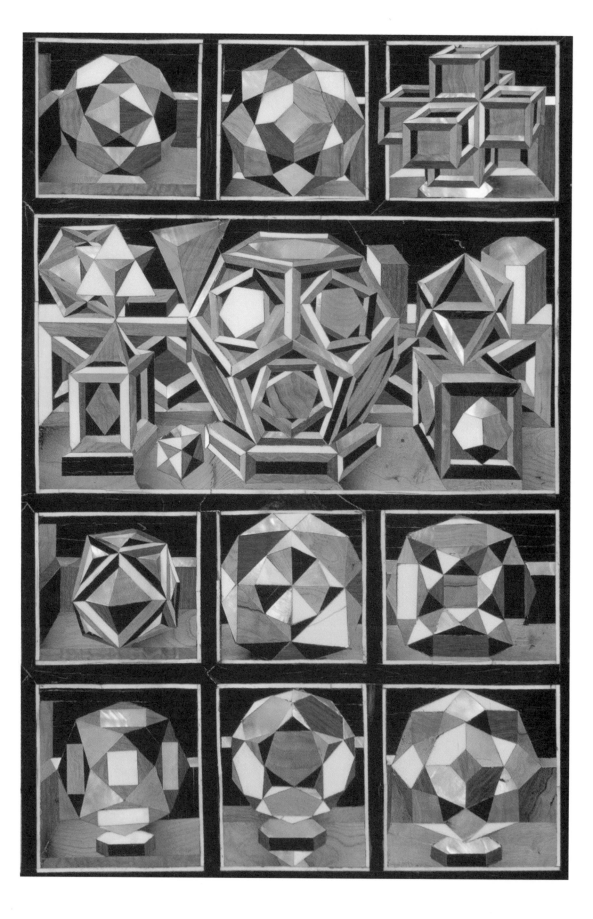

GEOMETRY & ART

DAVID WADE

How Mathematics transformed Art during the Renaissance

Shelter Harbor Press

New York

Shelter Harbor Press
603 West 115th Street Suite 163
New York, New York 10025

This edition published by Shelter Harbor Press
by arrangement with Alexian Limited

© 2017 Design and layout by Alexian Limited
© 2017 Text David Wade

Design: Roger Walton Studio
Picture Research: Susannah Stone

Library of Congress Cataloging-in-Publication
Data available on file.

For sales, please contact info@
shelterharborpress.com

ISBN: 978-1-62795-105-0

Publisher's note: While every effort has been
made to ensure that the information herein is
complete and accurate, the publisher and author
make no representations or warranties either
expressed or implied of any kind with respect to
this book to the reader. Neither the author nor
the publisher shall be liable or responsible for
any damage, loss, or expense of any kind arising
out of information contained in the book. The
thoughts or opinions expressed in this book
represent the personal views of the author and
not necessarily those of the publisher.

Printed and bound in China

10 9 8 7 6 5 4 3 2 1

Page 2: Detail from a 16th century
German Intarsia cabinet; Nuremberg.

CONTENTS

AUTHOR'S NOTE

The history of Art is intimately linked to the history of Ideas, and both have common ground in the human capacity for invention and imagination. Art has always responded to myth and religion where its role has been to portray, celebrate and reinforce belief, but this book is concerned with an influence of a rather different kind, that of a specific philosophical tradition, namely Platonism.

The concepts and principles of this philosophical tradition, with its origins deep in the Greek world of the 5th and 6th centuries BC, have exerted an incalculable influence on Western thought, to the extent that they have been completely absorbed into its core cultural attitudes. These ideas were truly foundational. However, although it was extraordinarily influential as a philosophy, the term 'Platonism' came to apply to a broad range of philosophical speculations, with a chequered history of their own – not all of which are entirely consistent.

So any study of Platonism must begin by plotting its origins and transformations over time, and the ways in which it came to leave its mark on European intellectual life. To do this I have felt it necessary to give an outline firstly of its basic precepts, then of its important contribution to the Later Classical World; its tenuous but persistent influence on Medieval thought; of its glorious revival in the Italian Renaissance; and finally how these ideas

were accepted and modified in their transition to the rest of Europe. As we will see, Platonism remained capable of inspiring and reviving the intellectual life and arts of Western Europe for centuries (despite the fragility of its influence during the turbulence of the Early Middle Ages).

One of the most important aspects of Platonism is its engagement with mathematics, and with Geometry in particular. Part of its great originality lay in the belief that Nature could be best understood through the abstract medium of number and measurement – an intuition that of course laid the foundation of Science. But these principles, which led it to give a high value to ideal formulations of numbers, proportions and geometric form, also exerted a strong aesthetic appeal. It was this aspect of Platonism that became a source of inspiration to artists from the very beginning of the Renaissance – in particular, the Pythagorean notions of ratio and harmonic relations as underlying, but at the same time existing above and beyond, the mundane world.

The interest in geometry that was revived during the Renaissance was associated with another field of enquiry, one that had been developed during the Islamic tenure of Classical Greek knowledge, that of Perspectiva, that is to say, of the science of Optics and the mechanics of human perception. Discoveries in this area were of equal interest to

scientist and artists alike – in fact the problems of creating a convincing representation of three dimensions onto a two-dimensional surface exerted a particular and sustained fascination throughout the Renaissance. This preoccupation clearly reflected the abiding spirit of the time, common to both the arts and sciences, which might be characterised as a drive to explore and grasp reality. Comprehension and measurement of every aspect of the land below and the skies above became an integral part of this enterprise. Vision was extended with lenses; knowledge by the printed word; the sense of space by geographical and astronomical exploration; the sense of ratiocination by developments in mathematics. And artists made an association between these concerns and that most rational description of objects in space, Geometry. In fact, regular Geometric figures themselves became objects of fascination for some of the greatest names in Western European art, and in some cases became the very focus of artistic expression.

In common with all artistic fashions however, this emphasis on geometric form ran its course and came to an end in the early years of the 17th century. The vehicle on which it travelled, the Geometric/Perspective Treatise (of which we will hear much more) carried on – but principally to carry the grander visions of the Baroque, a style that tended to eclipse this earlier tradition. Many of the productions of this geometry-based art have fallen into obscurity, and have tended to be dismissed as unimportant by-products of the 'Mannerist' tendency. But my own feeling is that Renaissance Geometricism, particularly that of the group of artist/craftsmen based in Nuremberg in the mid-16th century, deserves re-evaluation.

At a time when Art might be characterised as being in a state of free-floating uncertainty, and when Euclidean geometry itself has been superseded in mainstream maths, the pure forms of these art forms project a timeless quality that seems to me to have as much relevance now as they did when first conceived.

David Wade,

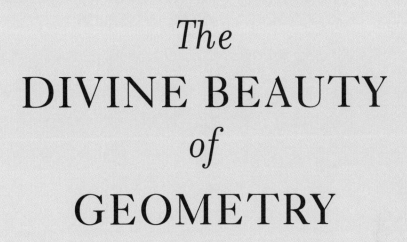

I

The
DIVINE BEAUTY
of
GEOMETRY

'Plato admired the basic geometry
of polyhedra so much
that he simply could not conceive God not using them.

Morris Kline, *Mathematics in Western Culture*

LEFT: *Westerner and Arab practising Geometry*
14th century manuscript.

THE CLASSICAL ORIGINS
OF A COMPELLING IDEA

PYTHAGORAS, PLATO AND THEIR HERITAGE

The potent idea that 'number is all', that mathematics underlie and are therefore the key to a deeper understanding the world, is usually attributed to the pre-Socratic philosopher Pythagoras. Pythagoras is a legendary and somewhat shadowy figure, about whom myths tended to accumulate – but he almost certainly did exist. He is believed to have been born on the island of Samos, and to have settled in southern Italy around 531 BC, where he established a semi-religious school of philosophy. Although the details of the earlier beliefs of the Pythagoreans are not known, it seems that they were much concerned with the study of music and

ABOVE: Pythagoras and Plato, as depicted in Raphael's fresco of Greek philosophers in the Vatican's Apostolic Palace. Plato carries his dialogue *Timaeus*, the primary source of his speculations on the nature of the physical world.

mathematics. Certainly their most enduring legacy lay in the discoveries that they made in these fields. According to Aristotle they came to believe that numbers and proportions were the primary elements of nature and focused their attention on instances where these were most apparent – in the ratios of the musical scales, for instance. They were also very interested in geometric figures, to which, as well as to numbers and ratios, they attributed mystical properties. In fact they seem to have believed that numbers and forms had a life and existence of their own, separate from the world, and they developed an elaborate cosmology in which certain of these were identified with Gods. Their speculations in the field of geometry were therefore bound up with a contemplation of the transcendent; constituting, as they saw it, a form of prayer. Importantly, for the future of European thought, their ideas retained their appeal. The school that was founded by Pythagoras endured for more than a millennium, and many of its precepts were taken up by Plato and incorporated into his own philosophical views.

The influence of this stream of thought is most obvious in one of the most important of Plato's Dialogues, the *Timaeus*, written in 360 BC. Following Pythagorean teaching Plato differentiates the physical, which is subject to change and decay, from the eternal, which consists of pure, changeless forms. The physical world is, however, derived from the eternal (although the details of precisely how this occurs are somewhat hazy), and is ultimately made up of elementary particles. These are of four kinds, corresponding to the four elements of the Classical world, Earth, Air, Fire and Water. The Elements, in turn, were identified with the first four regular solids: thus, Earth = cube; Air = octahedron; Fire = tetrahedron; Water = icosahedron. The fifth of these regular figures (which came to be known as the Platonic solids), the dodecahedron, was associated with the Cosmos itself. In time Plato's theories became so thoroughly bound up with the Pythagorean precepts that he had inherited that it was difficult to distinguish between them. But the linked notions of the importance of certain proportional values and the belief that geometrical forms were possessed of a timeless perfection, was a very persistent and creative one for both the arts and the sciences. In fact, the idea that arithmetical and geometrical forms could provide the means to

PYTHAGOREAN FIGURES

The Pythagoreans interpreted numbers as patterns of dots that were comprised of characteristic 'figures'. The most important of these was the *tetractys*, the triangular figure in four rows whose components add up to the perfect number ten (on which they would swear oaths). From this and other simple polygonal groups they progressed to cubic, tetrahedral, pyramidal and other three-dimensional series.

Aristotle later criticised the Pythagoreans for being number-obsessed, and clearly found many of their explanations far too contrived. Like numerologists through the ages they were rather prone to bend the facts to fit their ideas – 'If anything was lacking to complete their theories they quickly supplied it'. But despite the eccentricities of some of their cosmological views there was a great deal of substance in their theories, particularly the basic claim that mathematics is the basis of everything, and that geometry was the highest form of mathematics.

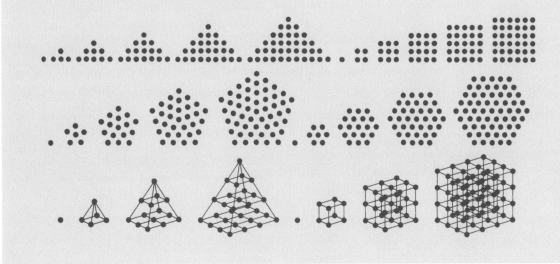

an understanding of the true nature of the Cosmos became a foundational principle of Western culture. This, after all, is the basic assumption of Science.

PLATONISM & GEOMETRY

Platonism is based in the first place on Plato's own writings, most of which survive, and on his and his followers teachings in the many succeeding schools of philosophy. This meant that although there undoubtedly was a 'Platonic' tradition, over time this did not amount to a consistent, coherent set of ideas. In fact Platonism (and Neo-Platonism) came to mean rather different things at different periods. [see ACADEMY side-bar]

The nub of Plato's thought persisted however. This was based on the notion of the independent existence of abstract concepts, and that the phenomenal world is merely a pale imitation, or approximation of the world of Ideas, which is eternal and perfect. Plato felt that these Ideas or Forms were not directly available to the senses, but could be determined only by a turning away from the 'shadow-world' of sense impressions towards an inner consciousness, and that this process could unveil the secrets of the Universe. Geometry was involved in much of this. Plato, like Pythagoras before him, was fascinated by the pure, precise relations that operated between geometric figures, particularly the solids, and came to identify these figures with notions of other-worldly perfection. His school, the Academy, famously displayed a sign that proclaimed 'Let none ignorant of geometry enter my door', and in his dialogue Timaeus (in which he lays out his cosmological speculations) he declares that 'God ever geometrises', and that 'Geometry existed before the Creation'.

There is a playfulness in Plato's writings, which are presented in the form of Dialogues (essentially debates), that allowed him to present a range of propositions that are not completely systematic. Although the ideas that are presented are thoroughly examined and questioned they are communicated through various interlocutors, that is to say, indirectly. Nevertheless, his preoccupation with the unreliability of the senses, the transience of the observable world, and the need for accurate definitions and clear hypotheses about it, contributed a great deal to the Western tradition of mathematical thought and to the scientific method.

*

In *The Republic* Plato asserts that 'Geometry draws the soul towards truth and creates the spirit of philosophy', and in *Philebus* he has his teacher Socrates explaining the particular relation between geometry and beauty – 'By beauty of shape I want you here to understand not what the multitude generally means by this expression, like the beauty of living things or of paintings resembling them, but something alternatively rectilinear and circular, and the surfaces and solids which one can produce from the rectilinear and circular, with compass, set-square and rule. Because these things are not, like the others, conditionally beautiful, but are beautiful in themselves.'

THE ATHENIAN ACADEMY

This school was founded by Plato in Athens in 387 BC. It is likely that during Plato's own time the school did not propound a particular set of doctrines, or have a prescribed curriculum, rather that lectures on a range of topics were delivered and discussed, with much emphasis on the dialectical method of logical argumentation. Judging by the content and scope of Plato's Dialogues, Mathematics, 'Natural philosophy' (proto-Science) and Politics were taught there. Aristotle and Heraclides were among the more illustrious of the early pupils (although the former went on to found his own teaching institution, the Lyceum). Later followers included the mathematician/astronomer Eudoxus, and the philosophers Arcesilaus and Carneades.

After Plato's death the Academy and 'Platonism' came to be dominated by innovatory, and more evolved, philosophical theories, beginning with Scepticism and then Stoicism. In the end a form of Eclecticism prevailed, by adopting what was felt to be the most reasonable aspects of the various contending philosophies, and in this form Platonism continued to be taught up to and during the Roman Era.

Although it managed to survive the Roman conquest, and the Athenian revolt in 88BC, the Academy's fate was very much determined by the political events affecting Athens. It was revived to a certain extent by the Diadochoi, the 'successors' of Plato, but was eventually closed by the Christian Byzantine Emperor Justinian in 529, in an act of repression that has been described as 'the end of Antiquity'.

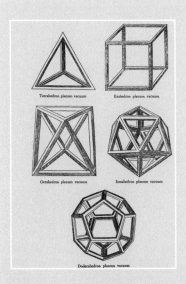

ABOVE: In his dialogue *Timaeus* Plato identified the four elements of Air, Earth, Fire and Water with his four of his five 'basic solids', which were in turn derived from two 'basic' right-angled triangles. The fifth and culminating solid in this scheme, the dodecahedron, represented the Cosmos itself.

THE PLATONIC CONTINUUM IN THE LATER CLASSICAL WORLD

As we have seen, Platonism (and Geometry) continued to be taught in Athens after Plato's death, and important discoveries continued to be made there. But after Alexander the Great in the 4th century BCE, Greece, including Athens itself, lost its importance. The towns of Alexandria in Ptolemaic Egypt and Antioch in Seleucid Syria, which had become important centres of the greater, Hellenistic Greek world, emerged as rival centres of scholarship, producing such outstanding figures as Euclid and Ptolemy. Whilst all were Greek-speakers, and had imbibed the Greek tradition of learning, many of these later scholars were not ethnic Greeks. The Greek world was now much vaster, running from Greece itself, through North Africa and the Middle East to Persia and as far as India.

Mathematics, particularly Geometry, continued to be a focus of investigation among the scholars of this cosmopolitan world, and its leading figures continued to make important advances. In 320 BCE, Aristaeus the elder, a mathematician who had attended the Academy, wrote a *Comparison of the five regular solids*, in which he established that 'the same circle circumscribes both the pentagon of the dodecahedron and the triangle of the icosahedron when both are inscribed in the same sphere'. This work inspired his near-contemporary, Euclid, who was to spend most of his life in the Egyptian

RIGHT: The Archimedean solids (from top left): truncated cube; truncated octahedron; truncated tetrahedron; truncated icosahedron; truncated dodecahedron; cuboctahedron; snub cube; icosidodecahedron; snub dodecahedron; rhombicuboctahedron; great rhombicuboctahedron; rhombicosidodecahedron; great icosidodecahedron.

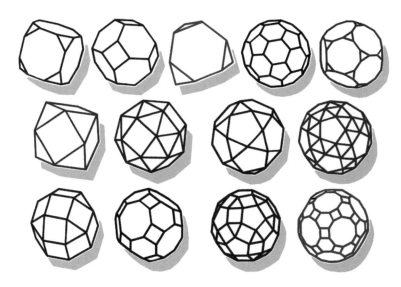

town of Alexandria. Euclid, who had himself been a student of a student of Plato, went on to investigate the whole range of plane and solid geometry in the same systematic, Platonic way – an enterprise that culminated in his *Elements*, the first comprehensive and logical system of geometry. In the final Book of the *Elements* Euclid explains, in eighteen propositions, how to inscribe the five regular solids within a sphere. To some later commentators this was taken as evidence that he meant his influential work as a sort of testament to their cosmological importance. The *Elements* was certainly one of the most influential textbooks ever written, and many of the greatest mathematicians of the Classical world made amendments and further advances on it.

The subject of polyhedra was of particular interest to another towering figure of this Later Classical period, Archimedes of Syracuse, Sicily. Archimedes thoroughly investigated truncated versions of the regular solids and in so doing discovered, and gave his name to, the thirteen *semi-regular* solids. Apollonius of Perga (262–180 BC), a long-time resident of Alexandria, was famous for his treatment of conics, but also wrote a treatise on the ratios between the

ALEXANDER, HELLENISM & THE ROMAN EMPIRE

By the 4th century AD the Classical world was approaching a serious crisis of confidence. In fact the Golden Age of Athens came to an end after the chaotic period following the Peloponnesian War when Philip of Macedon gained ascendency over all of the previously independent Greek City-states. His son, Alexander, having consolidated his father's conquests, took on the mighty Persian Empire, and after a decade of campaigning, managed to add this vast new territory to his Macedonian hegemony. These conquests included most of the Middle East, including North-East Africa, Babylonia and Persia, even parts of India. Alexander's conquests are legendary, but he did not live to enjoy them, dying at the extraordinarily young age of 32.

On his death these lands were divided up among the *Diadochi*, the successors (his friends, family and Generals). As can be imagined, this was a disputeful, acrimonious process – but it resulted in the foundation of a series of entirely new, Hellenistic Kingdoms, including Seleucid Persia, The Kingdom of Pergamon and the Ptolemaic Kingdom of Egypt. These acquisitions, in turn, were followed by a sustained period of Greek colonisation. In this way, and despite the break-up of Alexander's Empire, a new Pan-Hellenic civilisation was created. Greek civilisation and language was transplanted to all of these regions, primarily to the cities, in which vigorous new hybrid cultures emerged: Alexandria, in Northern Egypt was the most important of these

The gradual conquest of Greek territories by Rome in the 2nd and 1st centuries BCE led to the situation of 'Greek culture, Roman rule' in the eastern Roman Empire. Greek remained the dominant language however, and was widely spoken even in Rome itself. Rome, which was a highly militarised state, adopted a policy of aloofness towards its Greek dominions, but always retained a respect for Greek culture. Roman philosophy, art, literature and even religion, followed Greek models; most cultured Romans were bi-lingual. The eventual outcome of this fusion was a unified Mediterranean cultural continuum in which intellectual creativity continued to flourish.

dimensions of the icosahedron and dodecahedron. These discoveries were improved on by Hypsicles of Alexandria (190–120 BC), in a work that later became known as Book XV of Euclid's *Elements*. In the Late-Classical period speculation in mathematics and physics tended towards more practical applications rather than the purely theoretical. Even so, Hero of Alexandria (*fl.*150 AD) dealt with the measurement and relative volumes and sizes of polyhedra, and as late as the fourth century AD these matters were still engaging the interest of Pappus of Alexandria.

The mathematician/astronomer Ptolemy, also from Alexandria, is famous for his model of the universe, which endured until Copernicus. His brilliant (if misconceived) cosmological scheme, with its complex system of epicycles, was used to predict planetary motion until it was superseded by the Copernican model (which was actually derived from that of Ptolemy's fellow-Alexandrian Aristarchus).

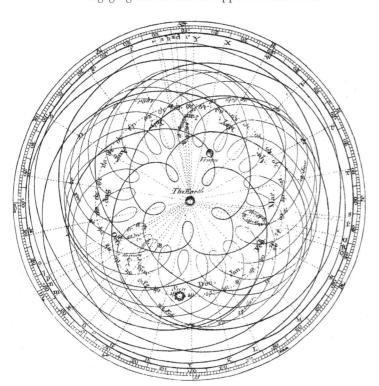

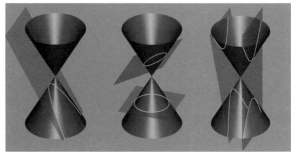

ABOVE: Apollonius of Perga, in building on Euclid's work on Conics, uncovered the properties of the important curves derived from conic sections: (left to right) the ellipse; the parabola; the hyperbola.

ABOVE: The geocentric planetary system that was established by Ptolemy of Alexandria in the 2nd century CE. It was an effective predictor of planetary motion but over time became ever more complicated to account for apparent anomalies.

RIGHT: The Ptolemaic geocentric Universe endured until the heliocentric model that was proposed by Copernicus in the 16th century. This is a late version, from the *Cosmographia* of the Portuguese cartographer Bartolomeu Velho, printed in France in 1568.

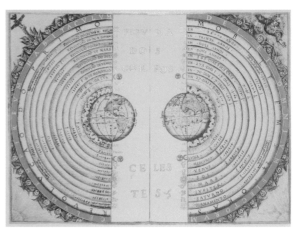

THE BYZANTINE & ISLAMIC TENURES
OF CLASSICAL GREEK KNOWLEDGE

In the 900 years between Justinian's closure of the Athenian Academy and the beginnings of the Renaissance in Western Europe, Platonism survived in three distinct cultural traditions – in the Byzantine Empire, in the Islamic world and, to a far more limited extent, in Western Europe.

By the 5th century AD the internal problems and external threats that had long been disturbing the Classical world reached a critical period, leading to the division of the Roman Empire, and ultimately the collapse of the West and the official adoption of Christianity in its East. But despite these momentous, and sometimes catastrophic, events there was a determination among some brave scholars to preserve ancient classical knowledge. In the event much was saved and Euclid, among others, was never entirely forgotten. The Roman philosopher Boethius (480–524 AD) for instance, living in the precarious conditions following the fall of Rome, dedicated his life to this cause, translating both Euclid and Ptolemy from Greek to Latin. Boethius regarded himself as a Platonist as well as a Christian and, in keeping with the spirit of the Platonic tradition, wrote tracts that associated geometry with music theory and astronomy, among which were dissertations on the regular solids. His philosophical views became a major influence on

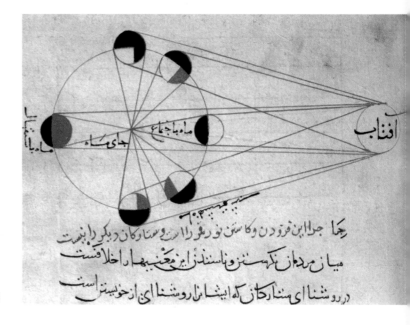

ABOVE: An 11th century illustration of the Islamic astronomer Al-Biruni's description of lunar eclipses; from his *Kitab al-tafhim*. Al-Biruni provides a thorough explanation of the celestial mechanics involved in this phenomenon.

the western Medieval Church, a beacon of rational thought during the Dark Ages.

In the Christian East, Byzantium was to remain a bastion of Greek civilisation for centuries to come. Classical science and literature continued to be taught and, particularly by comparison with the barbaric West, high levels of literacy and numeracy were maintained. Euclid's *Elements* remained

RIGHT: The Islamic world inherited and developed both knowledge and techniques from Greek, Late-Classical, sources. In this illustration from an Ottoman manuscript an astronomer calculates the position of a star with the aid of an armillary sphere and a quadrant. Much of this scientific knowledge was advanced by Islamic scholars and was later re-transmitted to Christian Europe where it greatly contributed to the development of European science and technology.

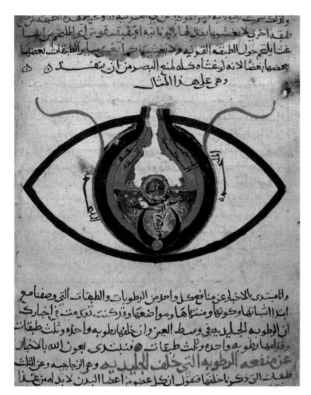

ABOVE: A 13th century ophthalmological diagram showing the anatomy of the eye, from a manuscript by the Arabic physician al-Mutadibih. Ophthalmologists enjoyed a high standing in medieval Islamic society and had developed a sophisticated range of surgical instruments.

familiar as a basic text, retaining its Platonic metaphysical associations; however these, along with other Classical philosophies, were incorporated into a Christian framework. In this setting geometry was seen as a means for a deeper understanding of God. The Byzantines, in a continuance of the early Christian Neoplatonic stream, were more concerned with such matters as the relation of the divine with the physical world than in science proper. Little original work was added to the technical aspects of the older texts at this time, but they were at least preserved. Constantinople itself became renowned for its humanist scholars who were regarded as 'the librarians of the world'.

The Byzantine Empire, although it endured for over a thousand years, was frequently under threat by external forces, from Latins, Persians, various Barbarian tribes and later, from the forces of Islam. The extraordinary rise of Islam in the 8th century had already robbed Byzantium of great swathes of its territory, but this initially nomadic incursion rapidly developed into a formidable, and rival, cultural entity. These early conquests by the Muslims, of much of the Byzantine Middle-East, introduced them to levels of culture and wealth that almost amounted to a second Revelation, and made an enormous impact on their own development as a civilisation. Effectively, Islam took over the vast geographical area that had been conquered by Alexander a millennium earlier.

When the Muslim conquerors had to administer their vast empire they naturally turned to Greek sources for knowledge of every kind. The urgent requirement for the resources that only a high culture might provide saw the establishment of a Muslim state-sponsored translation movement (see side-bar), and the beginnings of a sustained enthusiasm for available Classical texts. An atmosphere was generated in which scholarship was encouraged and Classical knowledge was soaked up like a sponge, giving rise to a thoroughgoing cultural reawakening that, in the second half of the 8th century, led to the translation into Arabic of the major corpus of surviving Greek medical and scientific works (including those by Plato, Aristotle, Galen, Euclid, Archimedes and Ptolemy). The enormous transfer of knowledge into this new, confident cultural setting had a catalytic effect, kindling a genuine interest in scientific subjects. Initially there was a continuation of Greek traditions of scholarship. Very soon, however, a confident and independent Islamic science emerged, producing valid criticisms and original extensions to this ancient knowledge.

The Islamic intellectual resurgence that followed was responsible for many important advances in mathematics (including geometry), optics and medicine, knowledge that was then spread throughout the Islamic world, even to distant Spain. The preservation, adaptation and subsequent transmission of this Classical heritage, together with that of Byzantium, was to have enormous consequences for Western science.

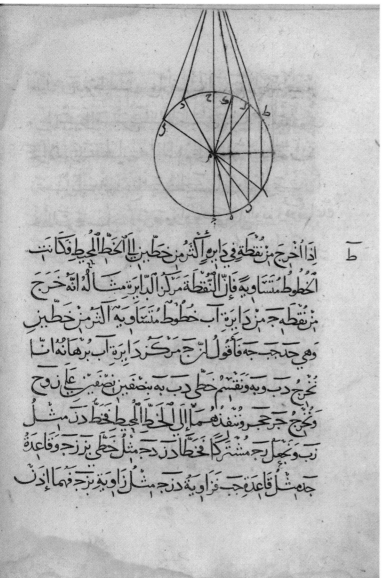

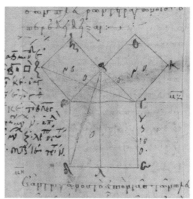

LEFT: Much of the corpus of Greek mathematics was translated into Arabic, beginning in the second Islamic century; a page from a manuscript of Euclid' *Elements* by Ishaq ibn Hunayn. This famous physician and translator resided in the House of Wisdom of Abbassid Baghdad, during the Golden Age of Arabic Science.

LEFT: The Pythagorean theorem, from Proposition 47 in Book 1 of Euclid's *Elements*, in a Byzantine manuscript.

LEFT: The same page of Euclid, demonstrating a proof of the Pythagorean theorem (that 'the area of the square of the hypotenuse is the sum of the areas of the other two squares') in an Arabic translation.

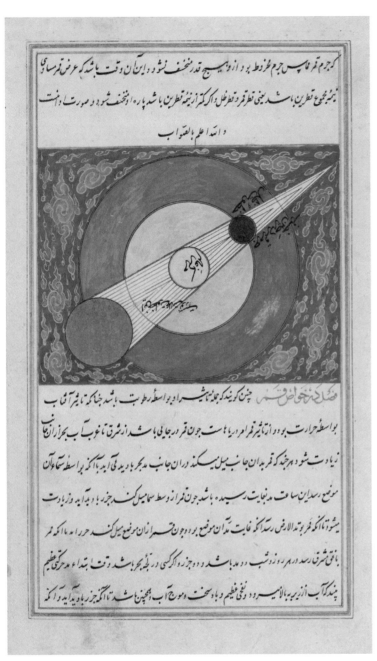

ABOVE: An illustration showing the method of calculating solar and lunar eclipses; from *The Wonders of Creation* by the 13th century Persian Astronomer and Geographer Zakariya al-Qazwini. Islamic astronomy was primarily based on Late-Classical, Greek sources, but it also incorporated Persian and Indian astronomical knowledge. There was a broad acceptance of the Ptolemaic, geocentric view of the Universe, which became the foundation of their own astronomic tradition, but Islamic scholars made significant corrections to this system.

THE HOUSE OF WISDOM

In 762 the Islamic Abbasid Caliphate, now ruling an empire that stretched from North Africa to the edges of China, founded its new capital at Baghdad in Iraq. It was during this period, Islam's second century, that they began to realise the enormous value of the Greek, Persian and Indian learning that was available from their conquered territories. Acquiring this knowledge became an imperative for the administration of the empire. The 5th Abbasid Caliph, Harun ar-Rashid, set up a school of translation, and original manuscripts began to be brought in from every available source. His son, al-Mamun, was even more enthusiastic and the work of translation (particularly of Greek scientific and philosophical works) was formally institutionalised as the *Bayt-al Hikma* (House of Wisdom). The appreciation and appetite for Classical knowledge was such that by the end of the 9th century the entire scientific literature of the Greeks was available in good Arabic translations.

In time, the *Bayt-al Hikma* became a research and educational centre and its scholars were soon making original contributions of their own in such areas as astronomy, optics, algebra and trigonometry. In this way Greek thought was not only preserved but broadened and advanced in its new Islamic setting.

LOSS & PARTIAL RECOVERY

When, in the 4th century, the Roman Emperor Constantine moved the capital from Rome to Constantinople the intellectual centre of gravity moved eastwards. The divisions between the separated halves of the Roman Empire were exacerbated with the fall to barbarian tribes of the western territories in the 5th century. The separation, politically and theologically, between the Greek-speaking East and the Latin-speaking West greatly increased over the succeeding centuries. The East managed to retain its cultural and commercial importance, and its capital Constantinople remained a vital strategic centre – but after the dissolution of the Western Empire its cultural life went into decline. The upheavals that Western Europe experienced between the 5th – 8th centuries, with its constant migrations and changes of borders were not conducive to cultural development (to say the least). Among what remained of an intellectual class there was little more than a sense of loss and nostalgia for the scholarship and arts of the Classical past – and the links to this glorious past became tenuous indeed.

One of the few surviving texts during these Dark Ages was Calcidius' partial translation of *The Timaeus* (in which Plato laid out his cosmological ideas – and related the myth of the lost civilisation of Atlantis). This work, together with Calcidius' commentary on it, was to be the only version of any of Plato's Dialogues available to Western scholars for almost

RIGHT: A 14th century illustration of a woman, probably intended as the personification of Geometry as one of the Liberal Arts, teaching Geometry to students. It is from a 14th century version of Euclid's *Elements*, that was originally translated by Adelard of Bath in the 12th century from an Arabic original.

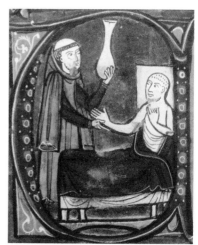

LEFT: An illustration from Gerard of Cremona's 13th century translation of Al-Razi's Treatise on Medicine. Al-Razi was a 9th century Persian physician/polymath.

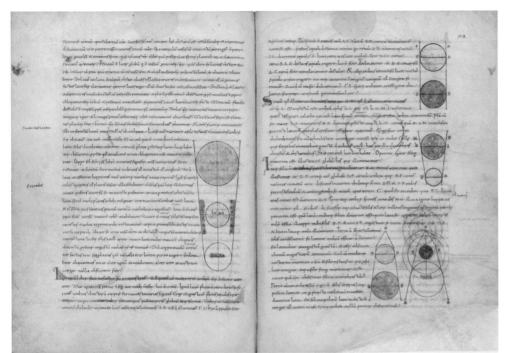

800 years. Interest in this commentary, which included some Greek astronomical observations, was revived in the 12th century, by French scholars

There were other determined attempts at reacquiring Classical knowledge during these difficult times, notably by Boethius (*ca.* 480–525 CE), a Roman aristocrat. Boethius, who is credited with devising the term *Quadrivium* (see spread 31a), made translations from the Greek into Latin of a number of books on mathematical subjects*, but his ambitions to translate the works of Plato and Aristotle were thwarted when he fell foul of his Ostrogothic masters. Sadly, there were no further attempts at translation for five centuries.

Over this long time-span those in the West with any knowledge of Greek became increasingly scarce, but during the more settled conditions of the 12th century a new trickle of important translations

from Greek to Latin started to appear and Antique scholarship began to re-emerge

Fresh contacts between Western Europe and the Eastern Greek-speaking world were being formed around this time, as a result of the tentative trade relations that Venice had established with the Byzantine Empire. A Venetian scholar, James of Venice, learned enough Greek to make the first Latin translation of Aristotle's Physics. Around the same time the Byzantine Emperor donated a copy of Ptolemy's *Almagest* to the King of Sicily where, because some Greek was still spoken, a translation was possible. Knowledge of the scholarship of the Classical past was still limited, but much more was soon to come, by way of the various points of contact that the Christian West had with its culturally superior rival Islam (see following).

* Interestingly, the inventory of Regiomontanus' library lists copies of Boethius' *Arithmetic* and *Music* (see page 55).

THE EARLY TRANSLATORS

During the early Middle Ages the Islamic world was far superior in the fields of science and medicine by comparison with Western Europe where intellectual life had been in decline for centuries. But by the 12th century Western scholars were becoming increasingly aware of the Islamic knowledge of the Classics and these were enthusiastically sought after by a range of determined scholars.

Arabic translations of Greek works had in fact become more accessible to Christians following the conquest of Toledo in 1085. This was a critical moment for the development of science in Western Europe. Under the rule of the Caliphate Toledo had enjoyed a golden age, famous for its tolerance and the coexistence of its Jewish, Christian and Muslim inhabitants. After its fall to the Christian King Alfonso VI it managed to survive as a centre of cultural exchange, supporting many schools of translation, which brought in individual scholars from many parts of Western Europe. Sicily was another important point of contact with Islamic culture, and the Crusades, for all their brutality, also created an awareness of the higher civilised values of the Islamic world. In fact, one of the chief stimuli for scientific, as well as cultural advancement at this time, were personal contacts with the Islamic tradition. These exchanges resulted in many important Latin versions of Arabic translations of Greek originals.

One of the most important of the scholar/translators was Gerard of Cremona (1114–1187), who travelled to Toledo in the mid-12th century where he taught himself Arabic, and was then able to take full advantage of the many libraries there. By the 12th century Spain and Sicily, which had long been under Muslim rule, now had Christian rulers but retained substantial populations of Arabic-speakers, which facilitated translation. Gerard dedicated his life to bringing an enormous number of important Classical works, and their Arabic commentaries, into Latin (an astonishing eighty-seven translations are accredited to him). Another monk, Robert of Chester, also travelled to Spain where he also made a compilation of works from Arabic sources which, in the following century, were used by the mathematician and astronomer Campanus of Novara (1220–1296) to assemble a reasonable Latin version of Euclid's *Elements*, a volume that became the most frequently used version right up to the 16th century.

Adelard of Bath (1080–1152) travelled extensively through France, Italy and the Islamic world and is recognised as drawing from each of the distinct schools of scholarship in these regions. He translated many important mathematical works from the Arabic into Latin, including those of al-Khwarizmi, and is thought to have been one of the first to introduce the Hindu-Arabic numbering system to Europe, although it was not widely adopted at this time. The distinction of the popularisation of this system is usually attributed to Leonardo of Pisa, known as Fibonacci (1170–1250), who encountered it during his own travels to Islamic North Africa where he recognised its utility and published his findings in a book called *Liber Abaci* ('Book of the Abacus') in 1202. This novel numbering system, together with the advanced accounting methods advocated in this book, had a profound impact on European thought and business practices.

There were many other notable individual scholars who made valuable contributions to the revival of Classicism in the centuries before the Renaissance proper, including Constantine the African, James of Venice and William of Moerbeke, but the long-held suspicion of 'pagan' ideas, and the Church's adherence to formal scholasticism were only gradually overcome. The move towards greater receptivity towards a whole range of new and revived ideas was reflected in both the Sciences and Arts in Western Europe (particularly in Italy) as the so-called 'Proto-Renaissance'.

THE CULTURE OF ANTIQUITY & THE COSMATI

The period of relative peace in Western Europe, which began at the beginning of the 11th century, paved the way for something of a cultural and economic revival in 12th. In Rome the natural direction of this revival was towards the recovery of

ABOVE: A *Cosmati* mosaic pavement.

the culture of antiquity, and there began a program of rebuilding with the ambition of restoring Christian Rome to the level of its pagan past. Although encouraged by the Pontiffs, the actual efforts to achieve this were enacted by the skilled artisans of the various Guilds and workshops that had come into being, virtually among the ruins of the ancient city. Prominent among these were various families of marble-workers, who became known as the Cosmati. As artist/craftsmen the Cosmati took their projects very seriously, studying the ruined buildings of Ancient Rome that were all around them, and finding their own techniques to construct elaborate mosaic pavements and other decorative architectural feature. There were examples other than in Rome for them to follow, including the fine Byzantine mosaic traditions of

Ravenna and Sicily, and the work of Muslim craftsmen, also in Sicily.

The Cosmati were sculptors and architects in their own right, and were also involved in the salvage of ancient material from Rome's classical monuments (many ancient sculptures in museums today still bear their marks). Rome and its environs was the principle centre of Cosmati productions, where many may still be seen, but their pavements were commissioned in Tuscany and Campania and surprisingly they even fulfilled commissions in faraway England (they created complex pavings in Westminster Abbey and Canterbury Cathedral, both of which still exist). This marvellous tradition flourished in Rome until the departure of the Papacy to Avignon in 1305, but their marmorari romani pavements continued to be made right up to the High Renaissance.

Renaissance artists were very fond of Cosmati mosaic paving, which feature in many of their paintings in Giotto di Bondone's Pentecost for instance, and Hans Holbein's The Ambassadors.

NEOPLATONISM AS AN INFLUENCE ON MEDIEVAL EUROPEAN ART

Initially, Platonism continued to be taught in Athens during the Roman era but it went into serious decline. In the early 5th century however, the Academy was revived by the Neoplatonists, a group of philosophers who regarded themselves as the direct successors of a tradition going back to Plato (although any actual continuity is doubtful). The term Neoplatonist is a relatively modern designation, and they clearly remained within the Greek rationalist tradition, but their focus was on the more spiritual aspects of Platonism. They believed that the rational Soul could have direct knowledge of Plato's realm of Forms, and in general their aim was to escape from the world rather than engage with it. This was a personal and intensely cerebral form of religion, without rites or communal worship, or prayer. However, many aspects of its teaching, particularly those of inner purification, were later incorporated into Christian theology.

Neo-Platonic philosophy was first developed by the Alexandrian Plotinus, who was described by a contemporary as 'being ashamed of being in a body'. The true self, in this view, belonged to the Intellect, which was eternal and independent of the body. This became an enormously influential philosophy in the Hellenic world, and in time Neo-Platonism exerted an influence on many early Christian thinkers.

Early Church Fathers such as Clement and Origen (both of Alexandria) attempted to wrest control of this Platonic legacy away from pagan philosophers, but it was St. Augustine who finally joined it to Christianity. The Alexandrian School survived until the Islamic conquests in the 7th century, and was to prove to be as much a leaven on Muslim thought as it had been on Christian beliefs

ABBÉ SUGER'S THEORY OF LIGHT

At some time around 1137 the Abbé Suger, began the reconstruction of the great Church of Saint-Denis near Paris, a master-work that is now regarded as the beginning of the architectural style known as Gothic. Fortunately, the ideas that drove Suger in this ambitious scheme are comprehensively laid out in two autobiographical accounts, both of which have survived. It is clear from these that the Abbé was deeply influenced by a much earlier writer, the Christian Neo-Platonist Dionysius the Areopagite (see side-bar). Inspired by Dionysius' Neo-Platonic ideas Abbé Suger developed an architectural philosophy known as *anagogicus mos*, 'the upward leading method'. According to this the Church building was to reflect notions of an upwardly-directed, light-infused Universe; 'the work should so nobly lighten the heart that they can reach the one true light'. Because of this, stained glass windows always held pride of place in Gothic architecture – the aim became to have as many, and as large, as technically possible. They were intended to move the viewer 'from material to immaterial things', to be a foretaste of Heaven. In the words of Abbé Suger – 'The dull mind rises to truth through that which is material, and in seeing this light is resurrected from its former submersion'.

Stained glass had been used sparingly in Romanesque churches since the 11th century, but the Gothic innovations of ribbed vaulting and flying buttresses created the possibilities for ever greater, ever more luminous Rose-windows. The form, which first appeared in Suger's Saint-Denis, is derived from an earlier style of window,' The Wheel of Fortune', but the received impression of Rose windows are entirely different. Whereas the Wheel refers to the relentless cycle of fate, constantly turning and changing for better or worse, the Rose, especially when filled with brilliant colour, offers transcendence. There may also have been a conscious reference in this mode to Plotinus,

ABOVE: A Rose-windows from Chartres Cathedral an ultimate expression of Abbé Suger's Neo-Platonic philosophy of *Anagogicus mos.*

who was much concerned in his *Enneads* with the unknowable centres of circles and spheres. Rose-windows, as the centre-piece of Suger's Neo-Platonic vision, were soon adopted by Cathedral builders all over Northern France and the form rapidly spread to England, Italy, Spain and Germany.

DIONYSIUS THE AREOPAGITE

Dionysius was a Christian Neo-Platonist of the late 5th century; it is possible that he was a pupil of Proclus who resided in Constantinople. His achievement was to reinterpret the entire canon of pagan Neo-Platonic thought into a new, Christian, dispensation. Dionysius (now known as Pseudo-Dionysius) did not claim be to an innovator however, but simply a communicator of a tradition. His theological treatises, though very influential, are deceptive, in that they are presented as coming from the Biblical Dionysius the Areopagite, a disciple of Paul.

The work of this anonymous author was translated into Latin in the 9th century by John Scotus Eriugena. Although in essence a forgery, it had an enormous influence on mystical Christianity in the medieval period, and indeed became a classic of western spirituality. Dionysius emphasised the transcendence of God, and the inability to capture his essence using language alone, although his own writing uses eloquent poetic imagery and an imaginative exposition of ideas. His theology was 'negative', in the sense that he tended only to affirm what God could *not* be – an approach that was widely adopted in later centuries.

NEOPLATONISM AS AN INFLUENCE ON ISLAMIC ART

By the time Muslim scholars encountered Greek thought, Christian Neo-Platonic ideas had long been a powerful influence in the Middle East. This meant that the earlier Islamic encounters with Greek philosophy tended to be through the lens, as it were, of these later doctrines. In time Muslim scholars gained access to original material and were able to discriminate and form their own versions of the Greek philosophies. Because of their compatibility with Islamic beliefs Platonism (and Neo-Platonism) became popular. The Platonic notion that the truly beautiful could not be conveyed by any work of representation or imagination, that it should express at least some of the quality of his 'Forms', seemed to chime well with emerging Islam aesthetic preferences. It is impossible to determine with any degree of certainty the precise ways in which Platonic notions of transcendent beauty influenced the modes of Islamic Art and Architecture, but the latter's preoccupation with symmetry, geometry, space, light and the dissolution of material form, which are present in even the earliest artistic expressions, all have a distinctly Platonic resonance.

Neo-Platonic notions that the Universe emanated from God in stages of spiritual, then material manifestation, had a particular appeal to certain Islamic mystics (*Sufi's*). These religious concepts offered the possibility that humans might be able, by developing appropriate inner knowledge, to ascend through successive stages of material and spiritual awareness to an ultimate, beatific, vision of Allah. There were problems with these ideas, particularly from those holding more orthodox beliefs, principally concerning the *emanationist* aspects of Neo-Platonism which were seen to conflict with *Qu'ranic* doctrine. Nevertheless, Neo-Platonic thought was absorbed into Islam theological bloodstream, notably through the influential figure of *Ibn Sïnä* (who became known in the West as Avicenna).

Unfortunately there are no biographical accounts of architects from the formative periods of Islamic art and architecture, let alone those of artisans – and unsurprisingly, the latter have left few documents detailing their work practices. As a result there are no indications at all that any of these were influenced by an overarching theory of any kind. The geometric patterns, arabesques and calligraphy that have played such an important role in this art were usually created within workshop traditions that were handed down through generations. The unwritten rules of this decorative canon, and the skills involved in creating it, would have become second nature to the artist/craftsmen involved and probably guarded as a trade secret in many cases.

Highly geometric decorative ornament, the consummate expression of Islamic art. **TOP:** An intricate *minbar* (pulpit) in fine woods and ivory from Egypt. **ABOVE:** Marble inlay from the tomb of *Itimud ad-Daula* in Agra, India. **RIGHT:** Ceramic mosaic panel from Fez, Morocco.

That a central concept of the Platonic stream of thought involved the association of Ideal Forms and Beauty, and that it was preoccupied with the purity of geometric forms as an expression of these concepts, can be seen to have had a strong bearing on the principle themes of Islamic art. With its pure geometries, perpetually playing out their symmetrical dances on the stage of the Euclidean plane, this genre seems quintessentially Platonic. Precisely how these original, lofty philosophical speculations were transmitted to those living at the artisanal level of society is another, possibly indeterminable, matter.

In later Islamic thought there were conscious attempts to expunge the influence of earlier and later Classical philosophies in favour of more orthodox religious views, but this earlier confluence of ideas – particularly the association of geometry with transcendent beauty – remained an influence on much of its art.

NEOPLATONISM IN ISLAMIC THOUGHT

Sometime in the 9th century an anonymous philosophical work appeared in the Islamic world that was to be hugely influential on the development of Islamic philosophy – *Kalâm fi mahd al-khair*, ('A Discourse on the Pure Good'). The 'Discourse' was Neo-Platonic in tone, and largely derived from two Neo-Platonic texts, the *Elements of Theology* by Proclus, and the *Enneads* of Plotinus. This work was influential because it appeared in an Islamic milieu that had already imbibed, indeed was thoroughly familiar with, much of the thought of classical Greek philosophy.

The philosopher/ mathematician al-Kindi (801–873) was the most important of the early Islamic philosophers, and the first to present the Neo-Platonism that was presented in the 'Discourse' in purely Islamic terms. Al-Kindi's version of Neo-Platonism emphasised the transcendent nature of Allah, but he was keen to stress the compatibility between older philosophical traditions and the tenets of orthodox Islamic belief. His mission was to reconcile their respective world-views.

Islamic Neo-Platonism reached its apogee however with al-Farabi (872–950), who developed a complex philosophy that brought together the emanationism of Plotinus with the cosmological systems of Aristotle and Ptolemy. Emanationism, which is strongly associated with Neo-Platonism, is a religio-philosophical model according to which all things are derived, or flow from, a First Principle, which in Islamic sphere was naturally identified with Allah.

Many other important Islamic philosophers were influenced by Neo-Platonism, evident in works that were themselves highly influential on Medieval European thought. These include – Avicenna (Ibn Sina), Averroes (Ibn Rushd), Al-Razi and Al-Tusi.

But in the Islamic world this stream of somewhat rationalist thought met with a backlash …

In the 11th century the *Mujaddid* ('Renewer of the Faith') Al-Ghazali, in his *'The Incoherence of the Philosophers'*, attacked the entire Greek philosophical tradition as a form of heresy – singling out the emanationist principles of Neo-Platonism as particularly incompatible with Qu'ranic texts. Although it was a rigorous philosophical criticism, Gazali's work marked an important shift away from rationalism in Islamic epistemology. However, by this time Classical philosophical attitudes had been thoroughly assimilated into mainstream Islamic thought – ironically even by Al-Ghazali himself, who used its dialectical methods in his refutations. And Neo-Platonic precepts continued to influence Islamic culture in many subtle ways. The otherworldly, geometrical, preoccupations of Islamic art, for instance, can be seen as part of this enduring legacy. The complex ideas of the religio-philosophical schemes of Neo-Platonism are unlikely to have been of interest to most Muslim artist/craftsmen, but their artistic traditions seem to have absorbed some of its broad notions by way of a sort of cultural osmosis. Importantly too, the mystical wing of Islam, Sufism, was deeply influenced by Neo-Platonism. Many Sufi orders subscribed to the idea that humans were able, by developing inner knowledge, to ascend through various stages of material, and then spiritual, manifestation, to an ultimate vision of Allah.

ISLAMIC SCIENCE & MATHEMATICS

The translation movement based in Baghdad's *Bayt-al Hikma* (see page 31) meant that the Greek achievements in the fields of science, mathematics and philosophy were completely absorbed into Islamic scholarship. The works of Plato, Aristotle and the philosophical schools that followed (Stoics, Neo-Pythagoreans and Neo-Platonists) were enthusiastically read by Muslims, and these ideas had as substantial an impact on theological and political thought in the Muslim world as they previously had in the Christian West. It was found that much in the philosophies of both Plato and Aristotle was compatible with core Islamic beliefs. The scientific achievements of the likes of Euclid, Archimedes and Ptolemy were also highly respected by Muslims, who regarded themselves as very much the inheritors of this tradition. Even in the Islamic world today, Aristotle is often referred to as 'the first teacher'.

The significant advances that Arabic scholars made on the Greek scientific knowledge that they inherited has already been mentioned; those in the field of mathematics are particularly impressive. This is in part because the early Islamic scholars were also able to draw on the mathematical traditions of cultures other than the Greek, including those of Persia, Babylonia and India.

Algebra (*al-jebr*) is high on the list of

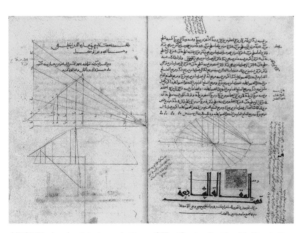

ABOVE: An Arabic translation of *The Conics* by the Hellenistic Greek geometer and mathematician Apollonius (262–190 BC).

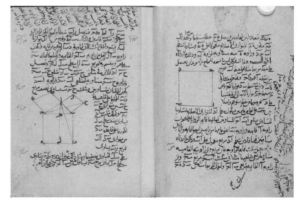

ABOVE: An Arabic translation of *The Elements* by the Hellenistic Greek mathematician Euclid (323–283 BC).

mathematical innovations emanating from Medieval Islam. Algebra, associated with the mathematical genius *Al-Khwarizmi*, was an original and revolutionary concept that greatly enlarged the scope of mathematics. It allowed numbers (both rational and irrational) and geometrical magnitudes to be considered as algebraic entities, and as such moved mathematics on from its Classical Greek origins which were essentially based on Geometry. *Al-Khwarizmi*, who gave his name to the term 'algorithm', was also responsible for introducing the decimal positional number system to the world. His successors, in particular *Omar Khayyám* and *Sharaf al-Din al-Tusi*, developed algebra to an even greater level of sophistication.

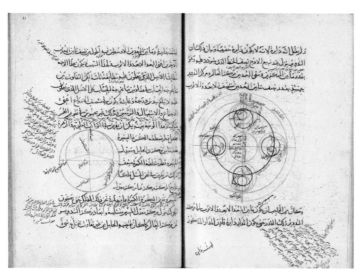

ABOVE: Pages from *Tadhkira fi'ilm al-haya* 'Memoir on Astronomy', by the 13th century Persian polymath Nasir al-Din al-Tusi. Among other achievements al-Tusi's wrote the first non-astronomical work on Algebra. His astronomical work greatly influenced Copernicus and he was the first to hypothesise that the Milky Way consisted of vast numbers of clustered stars.

IBN al-HAYTHAM

Few are so deserving of the term 'polymath' as Ibn al-Haytham, and few polymaths have produced their work under such straightened circumstance. Ibn al-Haytham was born in Basra, Iraq where he developed a reputation for applied mathematics. These skills took him to Egypt, where he gained employment with the Fatimid Caliph, Al-Hakim. An overconfidence in his own abilities led to an ill-fated attempt to regulate the annual Nile floods, but he soon realised the futility of the scheme. Fearing for his life at the hands of the notoriously capricious Hakim he feigned madness, but was placed under close house-arrest – where he remained for next 11 years. During this time, under constant threat of further and worse punishments, he wrote his *magnum opus*, the 7-volume Kitab al-Manazir ('Book of Optics').

When the mad Caliph Hakim died (under characteristically mysterious circumstances) Ibn al-Haytham was able to re-establish his sanity, and resume his scientific studies in more relaxed environment. He went on to write many more important treatises, on optics, medicine and astronomy, including the prescient *al-Shkuk 'ala Batyamlus*, 'Doubts concerning Ptolemy'.

IBN al-HAYTHAM'S *KITAB al-MANAZIR*
Originally written between 1011–1021, when the author was under house arrest in Cairo, this seminal work, the most outstanding of many on the subject produced in the Islamic world, laid the foundation of the modern understanding of Optics. It was brought into Latin, in the late 12th– early 13th century, by Gerard of Cremona among others, and had far-reaching influence in the West (as we shall see). Among many other of its highly original speculations, it described the correct process of vision for the first time - that is to say, of light rays emanating from an object to be received by the optic nerve. Ibn al Haytham's geometrical conception of place as geometrical extension, from which light

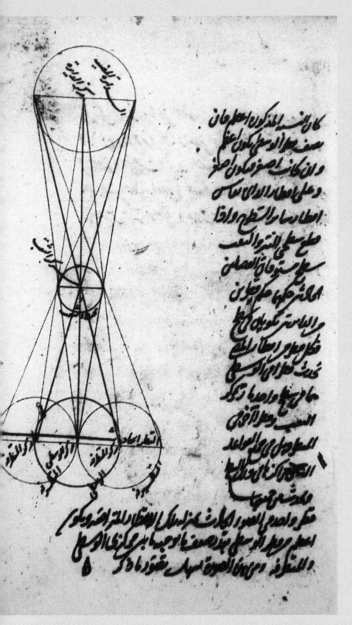

projected conically to the eye (*makhrut al-shu'a'*), later provided a proper basis for the notion of perspective.

Because of its rigorous treatment of the subject the *Kitab al-Manazir* it is now regarded as one of the most influential books in the whole of science. Ibn al-Haytham was a polymath who is credited with at least ninety-two books on a wide variety of subjects, including geometric figures. His theories on optics were based on a series of experiments with lenses, mirrors, refraction and reflection, as a result of which he came to be regarded as the 'father of modern optics'. His work in this area, which was originally based on that of Ptolemy, greatly surpassed that of his ancient predecessor, and he became the leading authority in optics for over 500 years. Ibn al-Haytham's methods, in which he constructed devices and repeatedly tested the results obtained from them, also introduced a new approach to scientific enquiry which was enormously influential in itself. His 'Book of Optics' was later used as a sourcebook by such early pioneers of Western science as Roger Bacon, Johannes Kepler, Isaac Newton and Rene Descartes in their own theories.

ABOVE: A diagram of a *camera obscura*, whose principles were first understood and described by Ibn al-Haytham in his 'Optics'. This drawing is by a later scientist Karmal al-Din al-Farsi who extended Ibn al-Haytham's pioneering investigation into optics.

II

THE REVIVAL
of the
LATIN WEST

*The great reawakening of science and art
that we now know as the Renaissance
was inspired and fuelled by translated
texts of classical antiquity.*

LEFT: Masolino's fresco *The Banquet of Herod*, 1435;
in the Baptistry, Castiglione, Olona.

FLORENCE IN THE *QUATTROCENTO*

Plato's philosophical works, together with those of his Neo-Platonist followers, were right at the centre of this great transfer of knowledge. As we have seen, the Classical heritage had not been entirely forgotten in the earlier Medieval west, but such knowledge that there was of its texts tended to be incomplete and second-hand. Greek was known to only a very few scholars and Latin translations were few and difficult to obtain. This changed in the later medieval period with a growing awareness of, indeed a positive enthusiasm for, rare Classical texts from both Byzantine and Islamic sources – but events in the East were soon to make a far greater volume of material available.

From around 1400, as a result of the disturbances caused by Turkish incursions into Byzantine territory, previously unknown Greek manuscripts began appearing in Italy. When Constantinople finally fell to the Turks in 1453 many Byzantine scholars fled to Italy bringing great quantities of manuscripts with them. These scholars, with their priceless volumes, were well received, particularly in Florence, where some went on to become intellectual celebrities. The bulk of the surviving Greek literature, which included classics of philosophy, mathematics, poetry and drama, suddenly became available. The influx of this wealth of knowledge stimulated the demand for translation, which in turn

promoted the discussion and dissemination of ideas – in much the same way that had happened in 9th century Baghdad.

Florence, with its leading figure the Neo-Platonist philosopher Marsilio Ficino (1433–99), became the centre of this great humanist movement. In 1462 Cosimo de'Medici, the *de facto* ruler of Florence, founded an Academy for the study of Plato. Ficino was appointed as its head and was provided with all thirty-six of Plato's dialogues in Greek, which he translated into Latin within seven years. He later translated and annotated the works of all the major Neo-Platonists, together with a collection of manuscripts from the 'Hermetic' tradition (see pg.202 for the *Corpus Hermeticum*). With all of these translations, together with his commentaries on them, Ficino's contribution to scholarship and humanism was incalculable, and he soon acquired an international reputation

The revival of interest in classical art and learning in Western Europe had in fact been slowly gathering pace over previous centuries, but the melting of frozen attitudes reached a flood in the Florence of the earlier 15th century. Many of the great changes that are associated with the Renaissance began there and the city continued to be at the forefront of advances in both the arts and sciences.

'This century, like a golden age, has restored

ABOVE: Detail of Ghirlandaio's *Zachariah in the Temple* shows Marsilio Ficino and other Florentine notables.

BELOW: 15th century birds eye view of Florence..

to light the liberal arts, which were almost extinct: grammar, poetry, rhetoric, painting, sculpture, architecture, music … and all this in Florence.' Marsilio Ficino, in a letter written to a friend, written in 1492.

HUMANISM

The intellectual movement that became known as Humanism marked a historical turning away from medieval scholasticism and a revival of interest in values and achievements of Classical antiquity. The rediscovered Classical texts that had been translated by Marsilio Ficino played an important part in this process, but from the beginning these texts, though revered, were not regarded as sacrosanct (particularly by comparison with the way that Scholastics had venerated Aristotle's philosophical works). The sheer volume of newly available material meant that Plato and Aristotle were reappraised, but also that many other non-philosophical texts of authors such as Archimedes, Ptolemy and Tacitus opened up whole new areas of literature and scholarship to debate. Moreover, with texts now available on such practical matters

THE MEDICI'S AND PATRONAGE

The House of Medici began their eventful career as Tuscan wool-merchants in the 14th century, but graduated to the banking business in the course of that century, and had established their own Bank by the end of it. By virtue of the family's astute (and ruthless) business sense, the Medici Bank rapidly became the most important financial institution in Europe – bankers to the Pope no less – through which the family were to soon able to acquire considerable political power, eventually bringing Florence itself under their control. The Medici's were as ambitious and acquisitive, and their lives were as turbulent, as many other of the great Italian noble houses of this period, but they stand out in that company for their extraordinary record of patronage, of both the Arts and Sciences. Despite their

ABOVE: *Lorenzo de' Medici*, portrait by Agnolo Bronzino.

relentless political ambitions, the Medici's created an environment in which Art and Humanism could flourish - their name is synonymous with the birth of the Italian Renaissance. The list of names of just the most eminent figures that benefitted from their largesse is impressive. In the Arts, Giovanni di'Bicci de'Medici supported Masachio at one stage of his short career and commissioned Brunelleschi for the rebuilding of the Basilica of San Lorenzo. Cosimo Medici sponsored Donatello and Fra Angelico. His grandson Lorenzo, 'The magnificent', was Leonardo da Vinci's patron for seven years, and also commissioned work from Michelangelo and Botticelli (in fact Michelangelo enjoyed the patronage of several members of the Medici family).

In philosophy, Cosimo founded the new, Florentine, Platonic Academy and appointed Marsilio Ficino as its head – a move that paved the way for a revolution in Humanist thought. In science, the Medici family were for many years the patrons of Galileo Galilei. Galileo, with his heretical views, enjoyed a certain degree of protection from the Church while in the Medici court, and tutored three generations of their children.

THE FLORENTINE ACADEMY

Ficino's Academy was based in the Medici Villa at Coreggi, just outside Florence. It became a centre where humanist members of the 'Correggi Circle' conversed regularly and informally, consciously adopting the style of the protagonists of Plato's Dialogues. The group was not organised in any formal way, and there is no complete list of members, but Cosimo Medici was an enthusiastic supporter of the philosophers and other scholars of the Humanist movement and many of these Florentine notables regularly attended the Academies lectures and meetings. Ficino's Latin translations (of Plato in particular) had made the works of Classical philosophy available and this had attracted scholars from all over Italy, and further afield, to Florence.

The subsequent influence of this scholarly movement was enormous. Ficino's philosophical proposals, which managed to reconcile Christianity with pagan Classical philosophy, were as important as his translations in generating interest in Plato.

Ficino's works were soon being read throughout Europe, and the example of his Academy was being replicated in other centres. Among other effects this stimulated a revival of interest in mathematics and in the natural world; study, debate and

ABOVE: Villa di Careggi, the Medici villa that was home to Marsilo Ficino's Academy.

enquiry flourished. Furthermore, new ideas and ways of thinking were rapidly diffused by the new medium of printing. A new epoch of European civilisation was being inaugurated, and the Academy was at the cutting edge of this movement.

as mathematics, agriculture, warfare, architecture, hydraulics etc., there was scarcely any aspect of life that could not benefit from this cornucopia of knowledge. The literary style of Classical works was equally influential. The form of the Dialogue, for instance, inspired a whole new literature that dealt with every imaginable topic, from art and warfare to mathematics and metallurgy. As well as stimulating academic and technological enquiry, Humanist attitudes brought in a new moral outlook, a sort of code of behaviour that involved self-control and moderation - and an openness to systems of thought such as Neo-Platonism and Hermeticism (whose texts had also been translated in Ficino's Academy). The invention of printing consolidated and propagated the Humanist outlook. The translations of Classical authors and Humanist scholars own texts became widely available – a development that was to have far-reaching consequences for intellectual life, firstly in Italy, but rapidly throughout Europe. It was soon expected that any educated man should have some knowledge and appreciation of Classical philosophy, as well as a reasonable grasp of the arts, sciences and civil law. Although, in essence, Humanism presented the ideals of a pagan civilisation to a Christian one, there was surprisingly little conflict with the Church. Indeed, many churchmen were themselves deeply influenced by Humanism; clearly, this was an idea whose time had come.

TOSCANELLI & HIS CIRCLE OF FLORENTINE INTELLECTUALS

The new Platonic Academy, founded at the behest of Cosimo Medici and headed by Marcilio Ficino, was the most important, but not the only focus of intellectual life in Florence in the later 15th century. Brunelleschi, the architect of the new *Duomo*, is believed to have been helped in this project by the mathematician/astronomer Pablo dal Pozzo Toscanelli who had his own circle of kindred intellectual spirits. Toscanelli himself, widely regarded as the most distinguished mathematician of his time, was an exceptionally wide-ranging and prescient thinker. He was a life-long friend of Nicholas of Cusa (an equally profound humanist thinker), Leon Batista Alberti and Ficino himself.

Toscanelli was the first European to propose that India, China and Japan could be reached by sailing west, and was consulted by Colombus before undertaking his famous Voyage. As well as a pioneering cosmographer, Toscanelli was a leading astronomer, making precise observations and calculation over a very long period. Very little of his published work has survived, but one short treatise, *Della Prospettiva*, concerned with his investigations into the optical properties of lenses, is believed to have sparked Alberti's interest in this subject. Alberti shared Toscanelli's enthusiasm for classical texts, especially those concerned with mathematical subjects. Both were concerned with measurement and proportion, views that Alberti laid out in his architectural treatise *'De re aedificatoria libri'*.

Nicholas of Cusa, who, like Toscanelli and Alberti, was a mathematician, dedicated two mathematical treatises to the former in 1445, and later produced a Dialogue, 'On Squaring the Circle', that took the form of a discussion between these two friends. Toscanelli was also in correspondence with the German astronomer Regiomontanus (see pg. 55), with whom he discussed the Earth's sphericity and the possibility of a sea-route westwards to China, discussions that eventually resulted in Regiomontanus's pupil, Martin Behaim making the first terrestrial Globe (around the same time as Columbus's famous voyage to the 'New World').

MEASURING THE WORLD:
RENAISSANCE COSMOGRAPHY

The Renaissance experienced a series of developments that were to have enormous implications for social change. The translation of the entire corpus of surviving Classical texts, as we have seen, was one of these, but then there were the extraordinary geographical discoveries as a result of maritime exploration (not least the finding of a whole New World), and the radical innovation of printing. Each of these advances occurred within the Renaissance time-line (i.e. later 15th early 16th century), each was in itself transformative – and of course there was a great deal of interaction between them.

The rediscovery of ancient mathematical texts, together with the revived interest in Plato, had generated a new enthusiasm for pure mathematics – and printing allowed an unprecedented dissemination of these ideas. Exploration and surveying called for improved methods of mapping and navigation, which themselves required new mathematical techniques – as did the increasing demands of commerce and trade. The demand for new accountancy skills to manage increased commercial activity led to a revolution in teaching. New 'reckoning' schools (*Scoulo d'abbaco* in Italy), championed by Humanists, were set up to provide

LEFT: This 16th century Flemish picture, *'The Measurers'*, was meant to show the practical values of geometry and mathematics in everyday life. The central figure is an instrument-maker with the tools of his trade, surrounded by objects that he has made (including a pivoted alidade, dividers, surveying-square, balance, sundial, quadrant and globe). Other figures are concerned with measuring cloth, weighing grain, surveying and gauging the contents of containers.

ABOVE: Hans Holbein's painting of *The Ambassadors* (1533) has its protagonists posing besides an array of state-of-the-art instruments that declare their Humanist, educated status. On the upper shelf of the table in this picture there is a Celestial Globe, a Torquetum, a Quadrant, a polyhedral dial and a cylinder sundial, (all of which are concerned with measuring the Heavens). On the lower shelf, besides various musical instruments, there is a Terrestrial globe and an arithmetic book by Apianus (see opposite). This is probably the most famous picture of its kind, but the inclusion of such items in portraits of notables was fairly common in the mid-16th century. Scientific, particularly Astronomical, instruments had a resonance for those wishing to indicate their commitment to the emerging, Humanist, world-view.

the children of merchants with the mathematical know-how that they would require in this milieu. The outcome, naturally, was a great increase in literacy and numeracy – which in turn, encouraged a supporting publishing industry.

Mathematics and Accountancy, which were thoroughly intertwined during the Renaissance, saw radical introductions during this period - the Hindu-Arabic system of numeration was adopted, and the decimal system gradually popularised by merchants (together with the important innovation of double-entry bookkeeping). Trigonometry, which had already been useful in navigation in the later medieval period, was mathematically formalised by Regiomontanus (*q.v.*) in his *De Omnimodis Triangulis* of 1533, and was further improved by Rheticus (Copernicus's pupil) in the mid-16th century. These advances in applied and theoretical mathematics, although radical, were paralleled by another, broader development, namely, a new emphasis on knowledge based on direct experience and rational observation. In today's parlance the Renaissance was more 'hands-on', which encouraged greater fluidity of thought, and theories were tested against actual experience – all of which amounted to a complete departure from Scholastic traditions of learning. It was these radical changes in ways that the world was viewed, understood, measured and exploited that

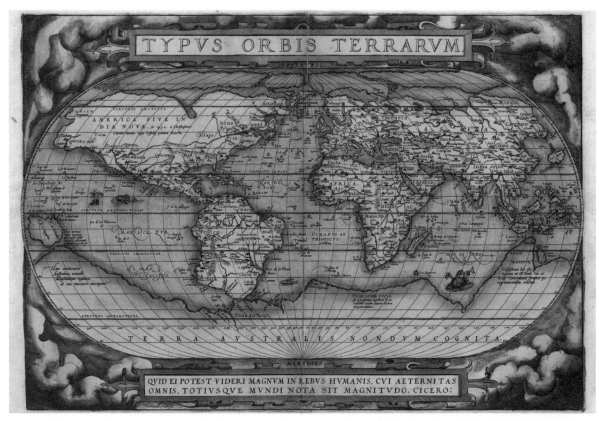

TYPVS ORBIS TERRARVM

QVID EI POTEST VIDERI MAGNVM IN REBVS HVMANIS, CVI AETERNITAS OMNIS, TOTIVSQVE MVNDI NOTA SIT MAGNITVDO. CICERO:

ABOVE: There was a great enthusiasm for cartography in 16th century Europe, almost amounting to a craze. This meant that by the third quarter of this century reliable printed maps were commonplace: Abraham Oretelius' World-map 1570.

fully justify the other label attached to this period, 'Early Modern'.

SCIENTIFIC INSTRUMENTATION

'Cosmography', in the sense that it was used at the time of the Renaissance, included astronomy, navigation, cartography, surveying and time-keeping – each of which were greatly improved during this period as a result of sustained advances in both mathematics and scientific instrumentation. In the early 16th century, following the discovery of the New World, the first whole-world maps (and Globes) began to appear, and by the middle of the century Gerardus Mercator had devised his famous projection. Such was the speed of the take-up of this new knowledge that by the third quarter of the century reliable printed maps of the world were commonplace. Theoretical and practical geometry played an important role in all of these advances. The voyages, and mapping, of the world that began in earnest in the 'Age of Discovery' promoted major improvements in cartography, resulting in charts that were sophisticated enough for use by Merchant shipping in their deep-sea voyages to the Americas and the Indies. Navigational instruments such as the Astrolabe and Compass were also improved, and printed treatises on navigation (such as de Albacar's *Breve Compendio de la Sphera y la Arte de Navegar*, 1551) became invaluable aids in disseminating information to voyagers. The effects of exploration were dramatic; exotic food-plants and other commodities (silks, porcelain, spices) began to appear in greater quantities than ever before, causing the entire focus of trade to move from the Mediterranean to Western Europe – ports such as Antwerp soon became the wealthiest cities in the world.

Measured by their effect on the common view of the world, the advances in Astronomy during the Renaissance were even more far-reaching. The publication of Copernicus' Sun-centred cosmology in 1543 was a critical event, and is frequently taken as the moment of transition from the medieval to the modern era. Regiomontanus (1436–1476), who is generally credited with having set the agenda for this and other aspects of the revolution in 16th century Astronomy, also developed trigonometry (the tables of sines and tangents he composed were extremely useful to Copernicus and Tycho Brahe among others). This brilliant scholar certainly measured up to the Renaissance notion of *Uomo Universalis*, since he also personally constructed an improved astrolabe and an armillary sphere.

*

The greater interest in acquiring practical knowledge of the world during the Renaissance went hand-in-hand with a whole range of important technological developments. The translations of classical texts on husbandry, drainage and irrigation, for example, encouraged a new enthusiasm for the cultivation of estates. There was a similar revival of interest in gardening, which was also supported by reference to classical precepts. As we have seen, improved techniques of surveying had a great impact on the way that the world was viewed – not least in facilitating the exploitation of natural resources

– in such areas as forestry and the extraction of minerals. For better or worse, one of the primary characteristics of the Renaissance was an awakening of the intellectual impulse to measure and explore the natural world.

FRISIUS & TRANGULATION

In 1529 the multi-talented Dutchman Gemma Frisius* published a corrected version of Apianus's *Cosmographia*, just five years after its original publication. The corrections were to the maps of the Americas – important, since it was now realised that these lands were comprised of not one, but two new continents. But Frisius may also have believed that this work, a general introduction to Geography, Astronomy, Surveying and their associated mathematical instruments, could have a wider appeal *and* could promote the sale of the technical/mathematical instruments made in his own workshop. His intuition proved to be correct. The revised version of *Cosmographia* sold very well indeed, running eventually to thirty-two editions in many different languages, becoming the most popular mathematical textbook of the 16th century.

But the new editions of this book had a further claim to fame, because Frisius used its pages to announce his new method of Triangulation. Triangulation, which allows a point to be fixed on a landscape using just one known side and two known angles, was not an entirely novel method of area measurement, but through Frisius's detailed exposition it went on to become the standard technique in Surveying.

* Gemma Frisius (1508 – 1555) was a philosopher/mathematician, a physician, a cartographer and globe-maker, and a maker of surveying instruments.

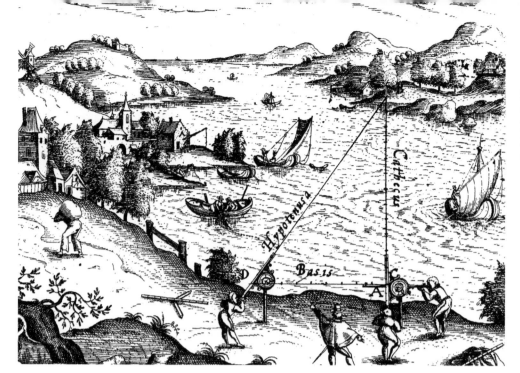

LEFT: Measuring the width of a river by triangulation. Levinus Hulsius (1546–1606).

Although far less striking than other mathematically-based Renaissance discoveries, the principles of topographical survey by triangulation, and the instruments developed to implement the technique, were every bit as transformational. The success of *Cosmographia* meant that Frisius's ideas were widely disseminated – with their capacity to throw a net over a landscape and measure huge areas from a distance, without contact, the idea had an almost magical appeal. But it was also intensely practical. Triangulated surveys went on to reveal the exact proximities of cities to each other, and then, for the first time, the true geographic relationships of entire regions. It allowed Princes to circumscribe their domains, Kings to map their countries, and Merchants to gauge distances. Importantly, being able to measure the world in this way changed human perception of it.

Later Renaissance mathematicians went on to develop Frisius's ideas – in England, Robert Recorde and John Dee provided additional mathematical underpinning for the method, and Leonard Digges

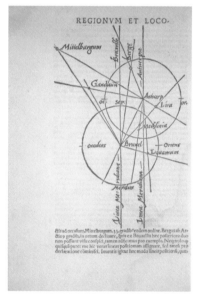

LEFT: Diagram of Frisius's method of triangulation. From the later, revised editions of Apianus's *Cosmographia*.

invented the Theodolite to improve its accuracy. In Denmark, the astrologer Tycho Brahe made a complete survey of the island of Hven (where his observatory was based) using Frisius's method. Gradually the whole of Europe was triangulated, later the dominions into which it had expanded, and the method eventually provided an highly accurate measurement of the Earth's radius.

FLORENCE & THE INVENTION OF PERSPECTIVE

The term *Perspectiva*, as it was used during the Renaissance, was actually broader than in its modern meaning. It was, in fact, the Latin version of the Greek ὀπτικά (Optics), and applied both to the physical aspects of light and the physiological aspects of vision, as well as the problems involved in the representation of spatial depth. Ibn al-Haytham's *Kitab al-Manazir*, which dealt with all of these matters, had, as we have seen, been in circulation in manuscript form in Latin translation since the 13th century, and available in an Italian version, as *Deli Aspecti*, in the following century. Al-Haytham (whose

name was Latinised into Alhazen) had conducted numerous experiments into the visibility of spatial depth, and his discoveries came to exert a profound and well documented influence on the course of European art.

Deli Aspecti was known to the Florentine sculptor and architect Lorenzo Ghiberti (1378–1455) who, according to his biographer, quoted from it 'verbally and at length'. Ghiberti has long been recognised as one of the most important of the early users of perspective, and he introduced the concept to his pupils, who employed the techniques to even greater effect. Among these were the painter Paulo Uccello, who had worked in Ghiberti's studio, and the sculptor Donatello (*c.*1386–1466).

The first actual paintings known to have employed the novel techniques of geometric linear perspective were made by the Florentine architect Filippo Brunelleschi (1377–1446), a contemporary of Ghiberti. Brunelleschi appears to have used perspective in his architectural drawings to demonstrate to clients how his buildings would look on completion. He is also known, some-time before 1425, to have produced two experimental panels, one of which, famously, was meant to be

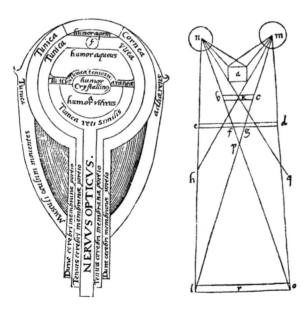

LEFT: Two diagrams from *Deli Aspecti* illustrating the mechanics of visual perception.

ABOVE: Saint Peter healing a cripple and The Raising of Tabitha. Masolino; the Brancaccio Chapel, Santa Maria del Carmine, Florence.

viewed in a mirror through a hole drilled in its centre to compare with its actual subject, the Florentine Baptistery. With these telling examples, Brunelleschi established one of the basic precepts of perspective – the notion that converging lines should meet at a single vanishing point on the picture plane, and that all the components of a painting should get smaller, in all directions, with their increasing distance from the eye. Others in Florence quickly picked up on this new theory, using it to marvellous effect – notably the painters Masolino da Panicale and Masaccio, both of whom were to employ perspective techniques soon after Brunelleschi's revelations.

A decade after Brunelleschi had produced his ground-breaking perspective paintings (which unfortunately have not survived), his fellow architect Leon Battista Alberti (1404–1472) wrote a treatise, *Della Pittura* (1436), specifically aimed at artists. This work described the new theories and methods of using perspective in some detail. Alberti was well equipped to impart this knowledge having been trained in science of optics in the school of Padua under the influence of Blasius of Parma (c.1374–1416), who himself had studied and taught al-Haytham's *Optics*. It is clear that Alberti's aims in *Della Pittura* were not merely to improve the techniques of painting by placing them on a more rational footing, but also to raise the professional status of artists above that of a mere craft, the role that they had occupied in the Middle Ages.

In the continuing chain of transmission, Alberti's pupil, Piero della Francesca, went on to elaborate on his masters treatise in one of his own, *De Prospectiva Pigendi*, which he illustrated with a series of diagrams and perspective drawings. It is

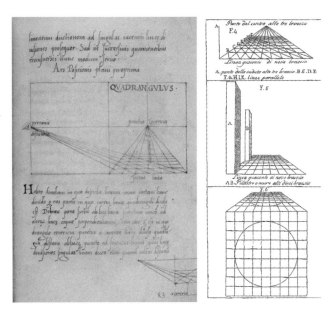

ABOVE: Two diagrams from Alberti's *Della Pittura*.

clear that Piero had come to regard the difficulties of realistic portrayal in terms of a solvable mathematical problem. This approach was very influential, as was the inclusion of perspective views of geometric figures in his book. His emphasis on the Platonic solids in this work effectively established their role as part of the repertoire of perspective treatises thereafter.

The plan and elevation constructions involving orthogonal lines (or 'visual rays'), used by both Uccello and Piero della Francesca, were particularly applicable for the portrayal of complex geometrical or architectural forms. The links between perspective and architectural planning were, as we have seen, already there with Brunelleschi, but the enthusiasm for perspective as a more realistic depiction of space in paintings, so characteristic of emerging early-modern attitudes, went together with requirements for accurate measurement of space in a more general way. As a result perspective

came to be associated with developments in the field of surveying, map-making and the instruments involved with these activities.

*

The earliest appearance of linear perspective in the written word appears in Leon Battista Alberti's treatise *Della Pittura* ('On Painting', 1435). In this he observes that 'a painting is the intersection of a visual pyramid at a given distance', as if the view through an open window were to be intercepted by a 'veil' across it. There is a clear indication here of Alberti's familiarity with Alhazen's theories ('He who looks at a picture in the way that I have described will see a cross-section of the visual pyramid') – and the first suggestion that artists might use a *Reticolato*, or reticulated frame as a drawing aid. He also puts forward a method of composing paintings that involved a defining horizontal line and the laying out of a base, rather like a stage, on which the buildings, objects and figures would be placed – the whole ordered by a grid of orthogonal lines to give scale to the various elements in the picture. This is, of course, the now familiar 'one-point construction', which introduced the revolutionary idea of a vanishing-point. It is clear from *Della Pittura* that for Alberti a knowledge of geometry was absolutely essential to the mastery of painting.

Alberti's successor Piero della Francesca, also emphasised the importance of geometry in comprehending the methods of perspective. In his own work *De Prospectiva Pigendi*, he too refers to the use of an 'intersection', which almost certainly meant a perspectival window of some kind (in fact these devices later became known as Alberti Windows). These new concepts spread very quickly. The use of the horizon line, the vanishing point and

INVESTIGATING THE CLASSICAL PAST

ABOVE: Filippo Brunelleschi (1377–1446)

The worldly, rationalising movement of Humanism, which led creative thinkers to investigate the nature of perception in a scientific way during the early Renaissance, was linked to a revival of interest in the buildings of Classical antiquity. The emergence from the cloistered outlook of the Middle Ages lead to a positive enthusiasm for every available aspect of this legacy. In this spirit Brunelleschi and Donatello undertook an extended survey of architecture in Rome, which included measuring the dome of the Pantheon. Their ambitious undertaking was for practical as much as nostalgic reasons – Brunelleschi went on to build his masterpiece the *Duomo* for the Santa Maria del Fiore, a dome that was even larger than that of the Pantheon itself. For his part, Donatello, after his thorough investigation of classical forms, introduced a new freedom and intensity into sculpture that was equally influential. According to Vasari, the author of *Lives of the Artists*, taken together 'these works were the means of arousing the minds of other craftsmen, who went on to devote themselves to this process with great zeal'. The 'process' he was referring to was, of course, the revival of Classicism, a movement that was eventually felt throughout Italy.

proportional foreshortening must have been fairly well established by the time Leonardo da Vinci encountered Alberti's system of perspective, very likely while he was still an apprentice in Verrocchio's studio in the early 1500's.

Leonardo himself became very involved in this subject. There are many references to it in the collection of thoughts and notes that became known as the *Trattato della Pittura*. There is a reference here to perspective as 'nothing other than seeing a place or objects behind a pane of glass, on the surface of which the objects are to be drawn'. It would seem that he experimented with a perspective window, in conjunction with a surveyor's rod, to create diminishing perspective – and recommended these devices as a method of training the eye. He also followed Alberti's suggestion of the use of colouring techniques, together with the appropriate, geometric, construction of shadows, to strengthen the illusion of depth. Leonardo's systematic approach to painting led to his uncovering of the inverse size/distance law, by which an object's apparent size is halved at twice the calculated distance, and reduced to a third when the distanced is trebled, and so on.

NEW WAYS OF SEEING:
LENSES & THE *CAMERA OBSCURA*

Developments in optics, in all its aspects, were a central concern during the Renaissance for both the arts and sciences. The aims of enquiry included both a better understanding of the physiology of vision and with the physics of light, an area of study which was bound up with the recent technical improvement of lenses, mirrors and other devices. By the later Middle Ages there had already been remarkable advances in Europe in this area. It can come as a surprise to learn that eyeglasses first appeared in Florence towards the end of the 13th century, and that by the 15th century these, and magnifying lenses, were relatively familiar items. The development of lenses,

ABOVE: Camera Obscura; Reinerus Gemma-Frisius, 1544. Frisius used a darkened room to study the solar eclipse of 1544.

particularly those used as eye-glasses is, however, somewhat obscure, presumably because the craft-skills involved were semi-secret. It is the case though that Ibn al-Haytham made reference to concave lenses and magnifying glasses in his 'Book of Optics', that this work was translated in the 13th century, and that usable glass lenses appeared in Italy in the following century.

In this work Ibn al-Haytham also refers to the theory behind the effect involved in what came to be known as *camera obscura*, and he also made the first analogy between this device and the workings of the eye. As a result camera obscura was fairly well understood by the 15th century. This effect, created by light passing through a small aperture into a darkened room, had of course been noticed throughout history. There had been many attempts, mostly wrong, at a scientific explanation for the phenomena, even in the Ancient world – notably by Aristotle. As well as an intriguing and useful tool for artists this contrivance was naturally of considerable interest from a scientific viewpoint. Leonardo da Vinci and Johannes Kepler both referred to it in their own writings on optics, and the mathematician/occultist Giambattista della Porter conducted a series of experiments that he revealed in his *Magiae Naturalis* ('Natural Magic', 1558).

GALILEO & THE MOON

ABOVE: Galileo Galilei 1564–1642.

Galileo's tussles with Pope Urban VIII and the Roman Inquisition are well known, but in reality Galileo was a devout Catholic and the Holy Office did not in fact dispute most of his scientific assertions. The opposition to his claims, leading ultimately to his incarceration, involved a clash of egos and vested interest rather than a simple Church versus Science battle. The Catholic Church as an institution was indeed having difficulty in accepting the new

Copernican, sun-centred cosmology, but there were already progressive elements within its ranks ready to make this change. The basic problem was with its adherence to Classical and Medieval speculation that had combined Platonism with Aristotolianism to create an Earth-centred cosmological scheme that divided the Universe into two distinct realms, the imperfect Sublunary region (beneath the moon), and the perfect, celestial Superlunary. Under the medieval Church this view had hardened into a rigid, unquestionable dogma. With his newly invented telescope, so primitive that some believed it to be a fraud, Galileo was able to see for himself that the Moon was far from perfect; it was, indeed, much more interesting than that – and the heavens were far more complex than the Church was quite ready to admit.

Interestingly, Galileo, who had grown up in the milieu of the Medici

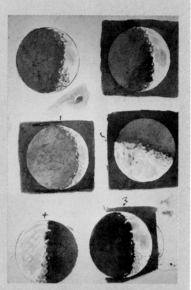

ABOVE: Galileo's drawings of the Moon, from his *Siderous Nuncius* ('Starry Messenger'), 1610.

court, had studied drawing at the Florentine Academy of Art and Design as part of his mathematical training.

The particular attention given to the study of optics during the Renaissance, and the advances in science and the arts that resulted, can scarcely be exaggerated. It was at the forefront of experimentation in an age of intellectual discovery, culminating in the appearance of telescopes and microscopes in the late 16th century. These developments quite literally introduced new ways of seeing, taking human perception far beyond the limits of the medieval imagination. When, for example, Galileo viewed the obvious imperfections on the surface of the Moon with his newly invented telescope the entrenched medieval distinctions between the 'sublunary' and 'superlunary', and the entire cosmological system associated with this, were utterly discredited.

THE GEOMETRICAL COSMOS

CIRCULATING PLANETS & SPHERICAL EARTH

Speculation on the arrangement of the Heavens and of the physical shape of the Earth was a primary concern of astronomer/mathematicians from the very beginning. In fact, theories that the Earth might be spherical, and the paths of the Planets circular, go back to the Plato and to his pupil the lesser-known mathematician/philosopher, Eudoxus of Knidos (c. 395–342 BCE). It is believed that Eudoxus attended Plato's academy, that his primary interests were geometry and astronomy and that his theories were strongly influenced by those of Plato. Unfortunately, none of the works of this philosopher survived the Classical period and everything that is known of his theories derives from commentaries by later writers – on whom he was a considerable influence. His was the first fully worked-out geometrical cosmology, based on a set of axioms derived from the Platonic perception that heavenly bodies are made of a more exalted and perfect substance than earthly ones. This astronomical arrangement placed the Earth at the centre of the Universe, with all celestial motion above it completely regular and perfectly circular. The *cosmos* was envisaged as a series of homeocentric spheres, with the central Earth successively contained within the invisible spheres of the Moon, Sun and Planets, a formation that allowed the embedded planets to move around the Earth in their perfect circular paths.

This model was adopted by Aristotle in his own cosmological speculations, which he laid out in his book *On the Heavens*. The Sun, Moon and Planets are themselves spherical in this scheme, as is the central Earth – although Aristotle postulated that this was 'of no great size'. He also conjecture that 'the ocean is one', and predicted that it should be possible to navigate from the Mediterranean to India. His theories on the physical sciences in general were so comprehensive that they dominated speculation in this field right through the Later Classical and Medieval periods. In fact it was largely due to the fame, influence and sheer scope of Aristotle's writings that the geocentric model, with its series of spheres, was so successful (and ultimately obstructive). But even in Aristotle's own time this model was questioned by at least one other important thinker - Aristarchus of Samos (c.310–230 BCE). Among other achievements, this amazingly prescient mathematician formulated a method for determining the relative sizes of the Sun and Moon. But he also put forward an alternative, *heliocentric*, cosmological model, quite different from that of Eudoxus and

ABOVE: A depiction of the Ptolemaic orbits in the form of an armillary sphere from the superb folio-sized cosmological atlas *Harmonia Cosmographia* by Andreas Cellarius. First published in Amsterdam by Johannes Janssonius in 1660, it was intended as a supplement to his earlier *Atlas Nova*. This volume, which also contains illustrations of the Tychoan and Copernican systems, is rightly regarded as the one of the finest productions of the Golden Age of Dutch cartography.

Aristotle. His scheme had the Sun and fixed stars remaining stationary, with the Planets, including the Earth, moving around this central, fixed Sun, and the Moon orbiting the Earth. This model, of course, is close to that which Copernicus put forward some 1,800 years later – and there may be a connection. It is known that Regiomontanus became aware of Aristarchus's theory whilst translating Archimedes' account of it, and it is quite possible that this knowledge was made known to Copernicus (who was taught by Regiomontanus's pupils), and fed into his own, revolutionary, heliocentric theory.

The Platonic/Eudoxian/Aristotolean model, however, was extraordinarily persuasive and continued to dominate Greek thought into the later, post-Athenian, Classical period. During this time pure abstract reasoning on matters astronomical was being supplemented by practical devices. The Armillary Sphere was one such; this invention is attributed to the Hellenistic astronomer Eratosthenes of Alexandria (276–194). Eratosthenes was a brilliant theoretical geometer and the first person to calculate the circumference of the Earth. His efforts in this were surprisingly accurate, with a less than 2% deviation from modern measurements, a remarkable achievement and an indication of the extent to which applied geometry was providing an accurate description of the physical world. His, and later, Armillary spheres consisted of a series of rings, representing celestial latitude and longitude, the ecliptic and equinoctial etc., which form a framework centred on a central Earth. Eratosthenes' device was essentially a spherical astrolabe, indicating the

ABOVE: An Islamic Armillary sphere: from Kâtib Çelebi's *The Book of Jihannuma*

motion of the stars around the Earth. This instrument was later taken up in the Islamic world, where, in common with much of that inherited tradition, it was further developed and eventually passed on to Europe as part of the great cultural bounty that gave rise to the Renaissance.

Archimedes, the most important mathematician of Classical Antiquity, produced an extraordinary number of treatises on geometry and mechanics, many of which became available to later medieval scholars through Arabic and Latin translations. As well as being a brilliant theorist Archimedes clearly had a very practical mind and is credited with the invention of a number of mechanical devices including pulley systems and the famous Archimedean screw. Around 225 BCE he published a two-volume book *On the Sphere and Cylinder* that detailed his investigations into the relative surface areas and volumes of these solids, and another work (unfortunately lost) *On Sphere-making*. Intriguingly, he is believed to have created a 'Planetarium', a mechanical model that demonstrated the movements of the Sun, Moon and Planets around the Earth (a device that later became known as an Orrery).

During his sojourn in Italy Regiomontanus read, and corrected, several Archimedean treatises in Latin versions. He would also have been entirely familiar with that most famous and influential book on plane geometry, the *Elements* of Euclid (*c.*295 BCE): Euclid's *Elements* were important not only for the systematic treatment of their subject-matter, but as an exemplar of the standards of mathematical proof and rigour. Regiomontanus also knew of the *Conics* of the Neo-Pythagorean Apollonius (3rd – 2nd Century BCE), and indeed had planned to print it before his

Classical perceptions of the relevance of mathematics to the study of both nature and art were probably the most important principle to have been revived during the Renaissance. It testifies to the potency of this concept that some of its greatest and most gifted personalities took it up (many of whom were also directly involved with a re-examination of the Platonic solids). The list includes Regiomontanus, Piero della Francesca and Leonardo da Vinci, all of whom truly were polymaths, in an age when such brilliance could span the disciplines of science and art.

Regiomontanus (1436–1476) is now seen as the most important astronomer of the 15th century, a pivotal figure who set the agenda for the revolution in astronomy that was brought to fulfilment by Copernicus, Kepler, Galileo and Newton. A translator of many important Classical works and founder of the world's first scientific press, he also made many important contributions to the study of geometry and trigonometry, and was involved in reforming the calendar for Pope Sixtus.

Regiomontanus was born in fairly humble circumstances as Johannes Muller, the son of a miller, near the small town of Konigsberg, in present-day Bayern. His prodigious talents were recognised early, and he entered university at the age of eleven. In common with other scholars who were dependent on patronage at that time he travelled, studied and taught widely, on both sides of the Alps. While still a young man Regiomontanus went to Italy where he learned Greek, and was much involved in the translation and publication of new editions of ancient texts (by Apollonius and Archimedes among others). He lectured in Venice, Padua and in Hungary, but later moved to Nuremberg, attracted by its reputation both as a centre for the manufacture of scientific instruments and of the new technology of printing.

Here he wrote a treatise on geometry, based on Archimedes' work *On the Sphere and Cylinder*, which included a section on the Platonic and other solid figures, in which he demonstrated their systematic transformation from one to the other. His work in this field laid the foundation for later geometers, including his pupil Martin Behaim (who built the first terrestrial globe), and the great Renaissance artist Piero della Francesca. Famously, his work influenced Columbus in the planning of his great voyage of discovery. Sadly, on his return to Rome in 1476, this wonderfully talented man fell victim to the plague and died at the relatively early age of forty.

LEFT: The frontispiece of Regiomontanus's *Epitome of the Almagest*, depicting the author sitting with Ptolemy beneath an armillary sphere.

untimely death. This geometrical treatise introduced the sectional curves now known as the parabola, hyperbola and ellipse. These were to become highly relevant to Astronomy; much later, in 1609, the orbits of planets were found by Kepler to be elliptical rather than circular.

Ptolemy (*c.*100–70 CE) like Euclid, lived in Alexandria in Northern Egypt, at a time when its famous Library was a flourishing centre of scholarship. Building on the work of his predecessors, Ptolemy developed a comprehensive cosmological system in his renowned *Almagest*. This Ptolemaic system, essentially a modification of that of Eudoxus, became by far the most influential of geocentric cosmological theories, enduring until the Copernican heliocentric model was published

in 1543. It had been known since Hipparchus (*c.*150 BCE) that the motions of the Sun, Moon and planets around the Earth were far from the uniform circular paths described by Aristotle and Eudoxus. Ptolemy accepted these older notion of the heavenly bodies' attachment to invisible, solid spheres, but his system was able to account for the annoying planetary deviations from regularity by an ingenious system of 'epicycles', i.e. cycles moving on larger cycles (thus preserving the credo of the perfection of the heavenly spheres). In this scheme the fixed stars moved on a celestial sphere that lay beyond the planetary spheres. Ptolemy also asserted the spherical nature of the Earth in the *Almagest*, and presented various arguments to support this proposition.

His other great achievement was an eight-volume work on geography, which amounted to a summary of everything that was known of the world at the time. Apart from physical descriptions and the relative dispositions of countries, the encyclopaedic *Geographia* contained detailed instructions on the methods of creating maps, and proposed a grid system that allowed specific geographic places and features to be assigned a co-ordinate value. With its geocentric assumptions, the cosmology of Ptolemy's *Almagest* was basically flawed, but it remained the most accurate predictive model for the next 1,400 years. The *Almagest* was the most authoritative book on astronomy throughout the Middle Ages and Ptolemy attained an almost mythical status. Regiomontanus, in common with all other 15th century European astronomers, would have been thoroughly familiar with the Almagest and other works by Ptolemy.

ABOVE: Claudius Ptolemy: from a fresco by Joos van Wassenhove *c.*1475.

EARLY EUROPEAN PERCEPTIONS OF A SPHERICAL EARTH: SACROBOSCO & CAMPANUS

The earliest extant records in Western Europe of any such elevated meditations as the shape of the world (or the cosmos) take us back to the time of Scholasticism. The term Scholastic applies to the academics of the emerging medieval universities – emerging, that is, from the Christian monastic schools of the Early Middle Ages. This movement began around the start of the 12th century, and was marked by intellectualism and the rediscovery of Classical learning; among other revelations, this involved the reappraisal of the works of Aristotle. Aristotle had long been known to scholars but translations of a much larger part of his *corpus* were now becoming available, including his *On the Heavens* (*q.v.*). One of the principle tasks of the Scholastics was to reconcile this knowledge with Church doctrines – which resulted in the double-edged distinction of making Aristotle a pillar of Christian dogma. In any event, it did mean that there was general agreement among medieval scholars that the Earth was spherical.

One of the outstanding scholars involved in early Western astronomy was Johannes de Sacrobosco (c.1195–1256). Sacrobosco was instrumental in introducing Ptolemy's *Almagest* and its evolved planetary system to Europe in his *Tractatus de Sphaera* ('On the Sphere of the World'). The *Tractatus* conveyed Ptolomy's assertion of the Earth's sphericity, but goes on to give convincing proofs of the fact. This

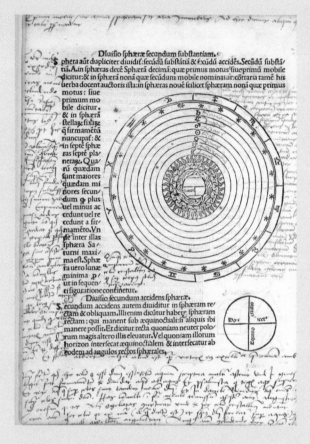

book, which also drew on translations of Arabic astronomy, became required reading for students for the next four centuries.

Campanus of Novara (*d*. 1290) was another important figure in the early history of Western European science. A mathematician and astronomer of the mid-13th century, Campanus is best known for his early Latin translation, from the Arabic, of Euclid's Elements – a version that became the standard for over three hundred years. He also produced a text known as the *Theorica Planetarum*, which provided a detailed account of Ptolemaic astronomy in Latin. In this he describes an Equatorium, which was an early astronomical device used to determine the relative positions of the Sun, Moon and Planets mechanically, without recourse to calculation. Regiomontanus is known to have acquired a copy of the *Theorica* in Vienna.

CELESTIAL SPHERES & TERRESTRIAL GLOBES

The invention of the Armillary Sphere is attributed to the Hellenistic astronomer Eratosthenes of Alexandria (he who calculated the circumference of the Earth in the 2nd century BCE). His, and later, Armillary Spheres consisted of a series of rings, representing celestial latitude and longitude, the ecliptic and equinoctial etc., which formed a framework centred on a central Earth. The Armillary was essentially a spherical astrolabe, indicating the motion of the stars and planets around the Earth. This instrument was later taken up and developed in the Islamic world.

In fact the entire Ptolemaic system, with its Earth-centred series of homeocentric planetary spheres (and spherical Earth), had been adopted wholesale by early Islamic philosopher /mathematicians and formed the basis of their own astronomical studies. Using observatories that went beyond those of the Classical world they made many great discoveries in this field but, as in Western Europe up till the Renaissance, geocentricism continued to hold sway. Essentially, there was a continuity of the Late-Classical tradition, albeit with many interesting advances. The techniques of spherical mapping and the earliest

terrestrial Globes were constructed here for instance (although none appear to have survived) – a body of knowledge that was eventually passed on to Western Europe.

The earliest known example of a terrestrial Globe in Europe was a version constructed by Martin Behaim, in Nuremberg in 1492. Behaim, who was a pupil of Regiomontanus, had travelled widely before settling in Nuremberg – as far as Portugal and West Africa. But his attempts at constructing a spherical world map were frustrated by the lack of geographical knowledge. At the very time that he was putting his globe together Columbus was on a voyage that was to radically and permanently change everyone's perception of Geography.

Columbus never realised that his discovered land was not Asia but an entirely new Continent, however, others did – and the great gaps in Behaim's 'Nuremberg Terrestrial Globe' were not long in being filled. By 1522 the Earth's sphericity was established beyond all doubt, with the arrival back in Seville of what remained of Magellan's voyage

ABOVE: A drawing of a geocentric Armillary used as a title-page for his *De Sphaera* by the German Jesuit Christopher Clavius.

of the circumnavigation of the world. By 1530 the enterprising Gemma Frisius (see page 44) was producing combined Terrestrial and Celestial globes in his Louvain workshop, together with an accompanying book, *On the Principles of Astronomy*.

This work provided a list and explanation of geographical and astronomical terms (such as latitude, longitude, poles, meridian, eclipses etc.), and gave vivid descriptions of the native peoples and plants of distant, many newly discovered, lands.

ABOVE: The Celestial Globe showing *Argo Navis*, a Southern constellation named after the ship used by Jason and the Argonauts in their voyage to find the Golden Fleece.

ABOVE: Martin Behaim's Globe, which was made in Nuremberg in the early 1400s. It uses the notions of Longitude and Latitude, which were part of the Ptolemaic inheritance, but incorporates all of the most recent discoveries of the voyages of the Late Medieval period (including those of Marco Polo). It does not however show the Americas. Behaim's sources were essentially the same as those available to Christopher Columbus, who never realised that he had discovered an entirely new continental land-mass.

THE EMBLEMATIC SPHERE

Whatever their practical utility, astronomical spheres of all kinds have always had an important *emblematic* value. Armillaries, in particular, seem to have acquired a wide range of symbolic meanings. From the late medieval period onwards they are frequently found in portraits of astronomers, astrologers and mathematicians, and became the recognised attribute of Astronomia, the personification of the art of astronomy (or of Urania, its Muse). They were also used in portraits of rulers to suggest worldly dominion, or in the depictions and emblems of saints, where they represented the contemplation of Heaven.

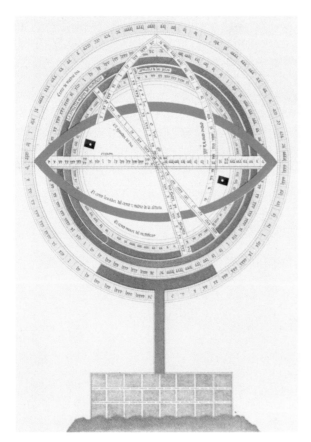

ABOVE: An illustration of an Armillary Sphere, used for demonstration; from *Libros del Saber de Astronomia* by D. Alfonso X of Castille.

In the Renaissance, particularly after the discovery of the New World, globes came to represent Universality, and were often found in pairs (a tradition that was established by the polymath/globe maker Johannes Schöner). For those who could afford them these were prized objects of distinction – and an indication of one's cultured, Humanist sympathies. The Medici's, naturally, possessed many globes, and in 1535 a pair of Celestial and Terrestrial globes were commissioned by the Habsburg Emperor Charles V. The fashion for globes spread and, through the new medium of printing, became more available during the 16th and 17th centuries. Nuremberg, with its traditions of cartography, instrument-making and printing, became the first important centre of manufacture; later this specialisation was taken up in the Netherlands.

In Tommaso Campanella's visionary Utopian tract *La Città del Sole* ('The City of the Sun'), which was written in 1602, the author describes the interior of his vast, centrally-placed Temple – 'Nothing is seen over the altar but a gigantic globe, on which all the heavenly bodies are painted, and another that shows every part of the Earth'. Many, like Campanella, had come to make the association between these depictions of the Heavens and Earth with more general aspirations for greater knowledge and understanding of the world.

PIERO DELLA FRANCESCA

Although best known for his paintings, Piero della Francesca (1415–1492) was also a mathematician with a particular interest in geometry, a preoccupation that increased in his later years. In fact the historian Vasari described him as 'the greatest geometer of his time', and he produced three books on the subject - *Libellus* *de Quinque Corporibus Regularibus* (a notebook on the five regular solids); *Trattato d'abaco* (dealing with algebra and the measurement of polygons and polyhedra); and *De Prospectiva pigendi* (a rigorous examination of the problems of optics and perspective). None of these were printed in his lifetime, but were placed, as manuscripts,

ABOVE: A detail from Piero della Francesco's *Nativity*

in the library of his patron the Duke of Urbino (where he had actually begun his study of classical mathematics). Piero is also known to have owned translations of the work of Archimedes and Euclid. Being used to the hands-on approach of a working artist, he shows a spatial, as well as an abstract mathematical interest, in the regular and semi-regular polyhedra. It seems very likely that he made models of these figures to assist his measurement and comparison of their respective volumes, and was the first to draw the Platonic solids as they should appear in perspective. He is recognised as a strong influence on the Franciscan monk

ABOVE: Piero della Francesca's *The Flagellation of Christ*, an enigmatic work showing the painters preoccupations with both linear perspective and proportional geometry. The division of the painting by a prominent Corinthian column (approximating a Golden section of the paintings rectangle) seems to demarcate two distinct times and places. The left presents the Biblical setting of the main subject; the right hand side is contemporary, possibly featuring members of the family of his patron, the Duke Federico da Montefeltro.

PIERO & ARCHIMEDES

Piero della Francesca

In the late 1450s Piero came across various translations of works by Archimedes that had been circulating in the humanist circles of Italian courts. He elected to transcribe one of these manuscripts, a compilation of seven surviving texts, and illustrated it with more than 200 drawings dealing with the mathematical theorems that it presented. The manuscript, which has only recently been attributed to Piero, is comprised of 82 folio leaves. The care and delicacy with which he lays out the geometric forms in this work confirms Vasari's observation of Piero as a 'great geometer'.

The treatises in this collation are 'On the Sphere and the Cylinder'; 'On the measurement of the circle'; 'On Conoids and Spheroids'; 'On Spirals'; 'On the equilibrium of Planes'; 'On the Quadrature of the Parabola'; and 'The Sand Reckoner'. This folio is now held in the *Biblioteca Riccardiana*, which is within the Palazzo Medici Riccardi in Florence.

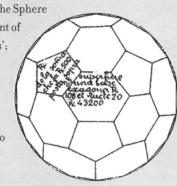

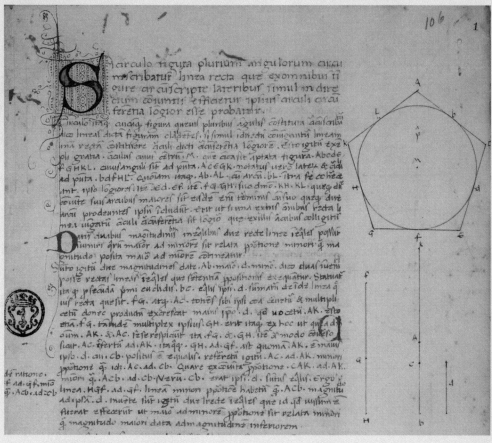

ABOVE: Piero's drawing of a truncated icosahedron, one of the thirteen semi-regular, or *Archimedean*, Polyhedra.

LEFT: Manuscripts of the works of Archimedes appeared in Northern Italy in the middle of the 15th century and began to circulate among humanist centres, including those of Florence. Piero della Francesca transcribed Latin translations of Archimedes works on geometry. This is a page from Archimedes' *On the Sphere and the Cylinder*.

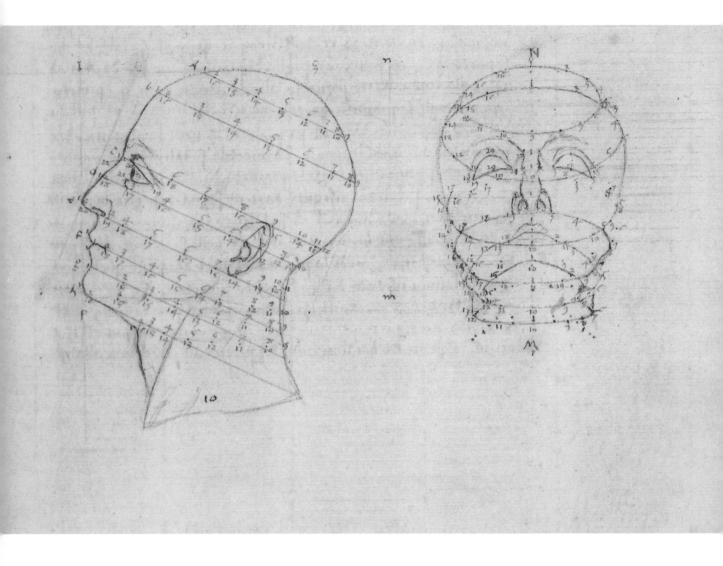

Luca Pacioli and on Leonardo da Vinci, whose contributions we will be dealing with shortly.

Piero's contemplative, geometrically structured approach to painting, evident throughout his career, was much influenced by Masaccio (and that artist's use of the vanishing point). His work exemplifies the imaginative use of space and perspective to produce the illusion of three-dimensional scenes.

ABOVE: In these drawings of 'Elevations and horizontal outlines' from his *De Prospective Pigendi* Piero della Francesca indicates the ideal proportions of the human head. To do this he adopts a system, possibly suggested by Alberti, of making sectional plans of the subject, which are then plotted via orthographic projection – a method that can, theoretically, create an accurate reproduction of the head at any angle.

PAULO UCCELLO

The Florentine painter Paolo Uccello (1397–1475) was also an accomplished mathematician. It is believed that he acquired some mathematical and geometrical skills from the Florentine humanist scholar Gianozzo Manetti, and that he may have been tutored by the mathematician and geographer Paolo Toscanelli, although little is known of this aspect of his career. He was apprenticed to the sculptor Lorenzo Ghiberti with whom he worked for several years, where he was probably introduced to the techniques of perspective, which then became a life-long preoccupation.

Various drawings by Uccello of geometric subjects have survived, including a perspective sketch of a *mazzocchio*, and a curious stellated sphere (both of which constantly reappear as motifs in the work of later artists). In 1425, Paolo was commissioned to work on mosaics for the façade of the Basilica di San Marco in Venice, where he stayed until 1431. Unfortunately, little has survived of this work, apart from one intriguing panel that shows a small stellated dodecahedron, (a figure that came to be associated with Johannes Kepler some two hundred years later). Taken together, these figures indicate a sound working knowledge of solid geometry.

BELOW: Paolo Uccello's pen and ink drawing of a *mazzocchio*, an exercise in the drawing of perspective, a subject with which the painter became increasingly obsessed: 1430s.

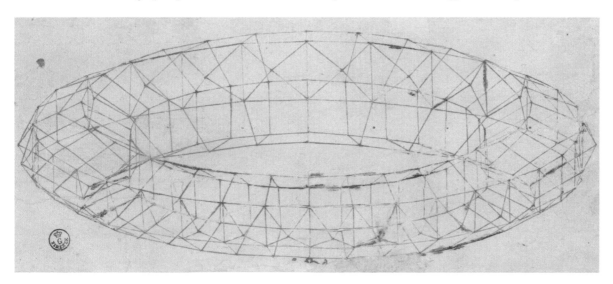

Uccello clearly had a keen, analytic mind and was fascinated by the problem of the reconstruction of objects in 3-dimensional space. Such paintings as 'The Miracle of the Desecrated Host' reveal an advanced understanding of the art of linear perspective, of which he must be regarded as one of the earliest masters. His foreshortened depiction of a fallen figure in the 'Battle of San Romano' is known to have created a sensation when it first appeared. It is likely that his perspective studies influenced Piero della Francesca and Leonardo da Vinci in their own studies of this subject. The historian Vasari makes rather disparaging references to Uccello's obsession with perspective (see side-bar).

ABOVE: This ink and wash drawing of a stellated sphere gives an indication of Uccello's mastery of perspective drawing. It is likely that the artist would have first made a model of this object, which went on, like the *mazzocchio* itself, to became part of the stock repertoire of perspective studies.

ABOVE RIGHT: A marble inlay from the floor of the Basilica of St. Mark in Venice, attributed to Uccello. This surviving example of the mosaic is remarkable in that it depicts a small stellated dodecahedron, some two hundred years before Kepler's 1619 description of this polyhedron.

OPPOSITE PAGE ABOVE: Uccello's *The Miracle of the Desecrated Host* epitomises the painter's sense of perspectival organisation. The subject, concerning host desecration, was a familiar preoccupation of the medieval Church, but is presented in a way that reflects Renaissance ideals of a universal harmony based on mathematics and geometrical proportion.

OPPOSITE PAGE BELOW: Uccello's perspective drawing of a chalice, in which he employs the same 'wire-armature' technique he used in the *mazzocchio* drawing on the previous page. In fact the mazzocchio form is incorporated into the upper section of the vessel.

VASARI ON UCCELLO

'He was solitary, eccentric, melancholic and poor. He would remain the night long in his study to work out the vanishing points of his perspective, and when summoned to his bed by his wife replied in the celebrated words 'How fair a thing is this perspective'. Being endowed by nature with a sophisticated and subtle disposition, he took pleasure in nothing save in investigating difficult and impossible questions of perspective. When engaged in these matters Paulo would remain alone in his house almost like a hermit, meeting nobody for weeks and months, not allowing himself to be seen. By using up all his time on these fancies he remained poor rather than famous during his lifetime.'

GEOMETRY, PROPORTION & *ISTORIA* IN THE *QUATTROCENTO*

There is a stylistic divide between the paintings of the late medieval and those of the earlier Italian Renaissance, the *Quattrocento*. Broadly speaking, this may be characterised as a move towards greater realism and spatial depth, and away from the flatter, hieratic qualities of the Italo-Byzantine style. The origins of this transition can actually be found a century earlier – notably, in the work of the *Trecento* artist Giotto – but these Proto-Renaissance developments were stalled by the advent of the Black Death. The inclination towards more realistic depictions of people, in settings that conveyed a sense of recession and internal depth, really got underway during the *Quattrocento*, and were a manifestation of the same, Humanist, impulse that was eventually to affect every aspect of European intellectual life.

The writings of Leon Battista Alberti made a significant contribution to these innovations – particularly his *Della Pittura* ('On Painting') which appeared in 1435. In this treatise Alberti made several recommendations to achieve a greater sense of naturalism, including the first written account of the use of the vanishing-point to achieve linear perspective (see box). He also stipulates that every element in a composition should have a rational relationship with all other parts, with the implication of a rational, ordered representation of figures, architecture etc. – ' This concord is realised in a particular number, proportion and arrangement demanded by harmony' – sentiments that clearly derive from a revived interpretation of the Platonic-Pythagorean tradition.

But in addition to emphasising the role of mathematics in painting Alberti advocated other techniques to enliven and dramatise a work. These include the use of light and shade to indicate volumetric modelling; the placing of figures in engaged groups (by contrast with the formal tableaux of medieval painting); the use of gestures and emotional expression in the *dramatis personae*; and a certain monumentality in the settings. All of these effects were intended to increase a sense of realism and the feeling that the events portrayed involved flesh and blood individuals (with what would now be called a 'back-story'), existing in a corporeal world. Alberti refers to this principle as *Istoria*. From this, the organisation of the figures, architecture and objects within painting should create an impression of a specific, instantaneous moment in real space.

OPPOSITE PAGE: Giotto's *Annunciation to St. Anne*, from his series of panels on *Scenes from the life of Joachim*, in the Scrovegni Chapel, Padua: painted between 1304–06. With its use of spatial depth and domestic realism his style anticipated later developments in the Renaissance.

GEOMETRY, PROPORTION & ISTORIA IN THE QUATTROCENTO

*

It is easy to imagine, looking at such pictures as Masolino's *The Healing of the Cripple*, Fra Angelico's *Annunciation* and Piero della Francesca's *The Flagellation*, the careful consideration that must have been given to the initial laying out and under-drawing of these masterpieces. We can be certain that during the earlier *Quattrocento*, in addition to adopting the new techniques of perspective, that the major divisions of the plane itself were given a great deal of consideration. The aim, although it was certainly not formulaic, was to convey a sense of three-dimensional depth in combination with the more intangible qualities of an ideal, proportional geometry. The use of harmonic proportions in the overall composition of paintings was intended to enhance this impression. The effect, particularly evident in works by Fra Angelico and Piero della Francesca, is of a formal, almost transcendent, elegance.

This concern with the proportional ordering of the plane was, however, short-lived. Painters of the next generation, such as Mantegna and Botticelli, were far more sophisticated in their use of perspective – it had indeed become the basis of their pictorial language – but they were no longer so focussed on the proportional geometry of planar arrangements.

These innovations were the consummate expression of the new humanist principles as applied to art. The focus was moving from the Divine to the Human, in art, as in society.

There is no doubt that these ideas were put into practice by many artists of the time and can plainly be seen in their works (particularly those of Fra Angelico, Andrea Mantegna, Piero della Francesca and Uccello). It is of course impossible to know the extent to which Alberti was directly influencing artists, or whether he was articulating a formal framework for tendencies that were in the air, that artists were already practicing. Alberti's contribution was an important contribution to the debate, but individual artists made their own individual responses to these stylistic criteria, and it is unlikely that they felt any sense of association with a 'movement' in the modern sense.

PERSPECTIVE & THE VANISHING POINT

Despite their admiration for Platonic notions of the aesthetic ideal it is unlikely that Plato would have approved of the attempts by the early Renaissance perspective theorists to 'deepen the illusion' in painting. Plato was opposed to the creation of, as he saw it, further levels of deception and error. He was, however, very conscious of the problems of perspective and the shortcomings of human perception, and concluded that only 'the arts of measuring and numbering and weighing can come to the rescue of human understanding' in this regard. As we have seen, the resolution of the difficulties in projecting three-dimensional space onto the two-dimensioal plane was indeed achieved through mathematical methods.

The first artists to introduce techniques involving geometrical diminution and the linked notion of convergence to a singular, imagined vanishing point on the horizon using orthogonal lines were Masacchio and Masolino da Panicale, who collaborated on various projects. Although he died at the age of twenty-six, Masacchio's work was enormously influential.

According to Vasari his frescoes were studied by all other Florentine painters in order to learn the new precepts and rules for painting.

Soon after this, Alberti, in his *Della Pittura*, brought out the first treatise to deal with perspective, which presented in a formal way various techniques to convey the appearance of depth in a painting, including the vanishing-point, shading, and the reduction of the relative size of portrayed objects, figures and buildings as they appear to recede into the imagined space.

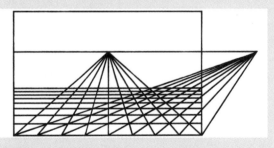

ABOVE: Leon Battista Alberti's perspective diagram from his *On Painting* Book 1.

RENAISSANCE 'CUBIST' TOWNSCAPES

In the medieval period the problems of depicting three-dimensional scenes were often side-stepped with axonometric projection, which, in essence, uses lines paralleled to the main axes. This technique is unsatisfactory on a larger scale where it produces obvious distortions of diagonals and curves, but is adequate (or at least less obvious), when used for separate elements within a painting. It was frequently used in portrayals of imagined or idealised cities in the background details of paintings. To modern eyes, of course, the naiveté of these gauche attempts to indicate solidity and recession can have an appeal of their own – but it was a problem that Quattrocento artists took very seriously. In the examples presented here, we can see both the artistic fascination with depicting the geometrical arrangements of buildings in towns and the gradual assimilation of perspective techniques.

ABOVE: Piero della Francesco: Detail from *The Recovery of the True Cross* (1450s).

ABOVE: Ambrogio Lorenzetti: Detail from *Allegories of Good and Bad Government* (c.1338).

ABOVE: Giotto; Detail of *Saint Francis Exorcising Demons from Arezzo* (c.1290s).

VOLUMES & PROPORTIONS

At a time when there was little standardisation of weights and measures, a facility for assessing quantities and converting amounts was a basic necessity for those involved in commercial transactions of any kind. In the 15th century the mathematics involved were essentially based on notions of geometric proportion – and this was the form of mathematics that was taught in the *Abaco*, (secondary schools) that were created precisely to meet this need. As a result, a large section of middle-class citizens, precisely those who would have been interested in art, were perfectly familiar with the sort of proportional geometries adopted by *Quattrocento* painters. As Michael Baxandall puts it 'Many *Quattrocento* people were quite used to the idea of applying plane geometry to the larger world of appearances because they were taught it for surveying buildings and tracts of land' (see Bibliog.). As mentioned earlier, the painter Piero della Francesca himself produced a mathematical treatise, the *Trattato de Abaco*, in which he instructs in the use of proportional mathematics to solving problems that might be encountered in trade and banking (his was one of many popular textbooks that dealt with the 'Rule of Three', a method of calculation essential to quantify proportional divisions of goods or cash).

The fact that the study of proportion was such an integral part of the mathematics of commerce meant that 'the painter could depend on his public's disposition to gauge', this was a geometry with which they were perfectly familiar.

ABOVE: Piero della Francesca's *Enunciation*, from the series *The Legend of the True Cross* in San Francesco, Arezzo: 1464. This painting is imbued with a stately sense of geometric proportion.

PREPARING A FRESCO

The techniques of fresco painting involved mixing pigments with fresh (*fresco*) plaster which then needed to be applied fairly quickly. Before this, walls were prepared with a rougher plaster and divided up into geometrical areas with 'chalk-lines' of *sinoper* (ground porphyry). Preliminary drawings were made on paper in the same proportions,* which were then transferred onto the wall using the squared-up method. This evolved into a more direct system whereby same-size drawings were made on larger sheets of paper (*cartones*), and transferred to the

walls by dusting black pigment through pricked holes. In both methods, further details were added by additional under-drawing in *sinoper* before the final painting (these are occasionally exposed as a result of damage or in the course of restoration). Clearly, much consideration would have been given to the initial division of the allotted area, and, as the new ideas of perspective were absorbed, of the placing of the vertical, horizon and orthogonal lines.

*By the late middle-ages high-quality paper was readily available in Italy.

LUCA PACIOLI

Luca Pacioli (1446–1517) came from Sansepolcro, the same small Tuscan town where Piero della Francesca was born. Piero was later to tutor the younger man in mathematics and to introduce him to the Duke of Urbino. Both were able to use the library of their noble patron, which was reputed to be the finest in Europe at the time. In 1494 Pacioli, who had in the meantime become a Franciscan monk and a travelling scholar, produced his *Summa de Arithmetica, Geometria, Proportioni et Proportionalità* – a summary of maths that was eventually printed in Venice using the new Gutenberg method. This work brought him a measure of fame – and to the notice of Leonardo da Vinci, who brought him to Milan, where he was to stay for some three fruitful years. During this time, between 1496 and 1499, he wrote *De Divina Proportione*, a book that was equally based on Plato's philosophical speculations, Euclid's geometry and Christian theology – all of which he related to the Golden Proportion in a grand, if slightly confusing, cosmological scheme (see following page). Leonardo, who was receiving tuition in mathematics from Pacioli at this time, collaborated with him on the book, contributing many illustrations, including an engaging series of 'skeletised' and solid versions of polyhedra. The 'Divine Proportion' itself was eventually printed and published in Venice in 1509,

and enjoyed immediate success. The historian Vasari, although he was writing some fifty years later, was rather scathing of Pacioli's work on the *Divina*, accusing him plagiarism, saying that he had lifted much of this work from Piero della Francesca, without giving the artist/mathematician full credit for it. Although this assertion may have some basis it does seem rather harsh; Pacioli comes across as a genuinely pious scholar and dedicated teacher. Soon after the publication of De Divina he made a Latin translation of Euclid's *Elements*.

This extraordinary man also has the distinction of having introduced the technique of double-entry bookkeeping, and is as famous for that – particularly in the world of accountancy, where he is regarded as a founding-figure – as for *De Divina Proportione*. It is a matter of interest that the Medici's were among the first merchant bankers to adopt this system.

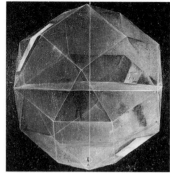

ABOVE: Detail of this painting showing a suspended glass rhombicuboctahedron, partially filled with water. Because of the delicate rendering of its complex reflections and refractions it has been suggested that Pacioli's friend, Leonardo da Vinci, may have had a hand in this part of the painting.

ABOVE: Illustrative page of Pacioli's *Summa de Arithmetica, Geometria, Proportione et Proportionalità.*

DE VIRIBUS QUANTITUS

In 2006 the mathematician David Singmaster uncovered a reference to previously unknown book by Pacioli in the library of the University of Bologna. This turned out to be an extensive treatise on mathematical games and problems, *De Viribus Quantitatis* — a huge compendium in three parts, dealing, respectively, with mathematical problems, tricks and diversions, verses and proverbs. It has been described as 'the first major manual concerned with teaching how to perform magic'. Among other things it gives instructions on how to perform card tricks, on juggling, fire-eating and other conjuring skills — the emphasis throughout is on puzzlement, performance and

entertainment. Pacioli, serious as he was in his mathematical expositions, clearly had a lighter side.

The *Viribus* was apparently put together over a ten-year period, begun around the same time that Pacioli was working on *De Divina Proportione*. He mentions his friend Leonardo da Vinci several times in the book (with suggestions indicating that he may have contributed to it), and thanks him profusely for his collaboration on the *Divina Proportione*. For some reason, probably to do with their both having to flee from Milan as a result of the French invasion of that city in 1499, the *Viribus* was never published.

DE DIVINA PROPORTIONE

Luca Pacioli created his masterwork *De Divina Proportione* in Milan between the years 1497–1498, and it was eventually printed and published in Venice in 1509. It is comprised of three sections that deal, respectively, with the Golden Ratio and perspective; the principles of mathematics; the rational system of proportion advanced by the Roman author and architect Vitruvius in his *De Architectura*; finishing with a treatise on the five regular 'Platonic' solids (which largely consists of an Italian transcription of Piero della Francesca's *De quinque corporibus regularibus*). Pacioli was assisted in this project by Leonardo da Vinci, who supplied its many illustrations and diagrams.

The book refers to Plato's cosmology in the *Timaeus*, and to Euclids *Elements*, making it clear that his dissertation rested on the bedrock of Classical notions of geometry. As noted above, he also depended heavily on the work of his former teacher Piero della Francesca. His originality lies in presenting these ideas in a clear, graphic and systematic form; the many drawings of three dimensional figures are the most striking example of this. Pacioli is known to have commissioned polyhedral models even before he met Leonardo, and it is very likely that many more were made to facilitate the drawing of solid and 'skeletised' figures that the artist provided for his book (59 in all).

The 'divine proportion', which Pacioli referred to as 'essential, awesome and invaluable, is a mathematical value that is now known as *phi* (see side-bar); in *De Divina* explores the relation of this proportion to the regular Platonic, and semi-regular Archimedean polyhedra. For Pacioli the interconnectivity in these geometrical relations clearly had mystical and divine connotations; as he says, it touches on 'a very secret science'.

PHI

There are many descriptive terms for this value - Golden Mean; Golden Section; Golden Number; Golden Ratio etc.; it is found in Book 6 of Euclid's *Elements*. It is simply where the section, or cut, in a given line produces two lengths that express precisely the same ratio as that of the larger part to the whole line (see below).

The ratio of the line A- Φ to Φ -B is the same as that of A-B to A- Φ

A ——————— Φ ————— B

This ratio, which was probably known to the Pythagoreans, is closely associated with 5-fold ge-

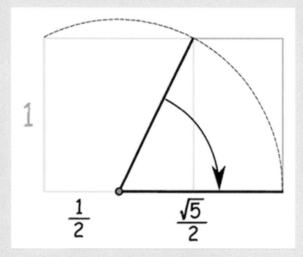

LEFT: This simple formulation, first given by Euclid in 300 BCE, defines the intriguing incommensurable value now known as *phi*.

$$\frac{1}{2} \qquad \frac{\sqrt{5}}{2}$$

ometry (the pentagon, the pentagram, the dodecahedron).

A rectangle that uses this proportion is known as a Golden rectangle, the proportions of which have been claimed to be particularly harmonic and aesthetically appealing.

ABOVE AND RIGHT: Pacioli's *De Divina Proportione* is extensively illustrated with drawings of polyhedra, in solid and 'skeletised' form, contributed by his friend Leonardo da Vinci.

LEONARDO & GEOMETRY

One of the most productive of the new attitudes that came with the revival of Classical culture and ideas during the Renaissance was the notion of mathematics, and particularly geometry, as an essential subject both for the deeper understanding of nature and as a proper basis for art. Leonardo da Vinci (1452–1519) was at the very forefront of this movement. As we have seen, he provided the drawings for Pacioli's *De Divina Proportione*, and his notebook drawings testify to a continuing interest in many aspects of geometry, proportion and perspective – including sketches of several geometric solids not found in Pacioli's work, including an entire series of regular and semi-regular solids.

Leonardo began to dedicate much of his time to geometry in his early forties. It is known that he had become familiar with the five regular and thirteen semi-regular 'Archimedean' solids (since they appear in the collection of drawings known as the *Codice Atlantico*), and that by the time he had finished working with Pacioli he had become so enthralled with mathematics that he neglected his painting – a contemporary observer noted at the time that 'the sight of a brush puts him out of temper'. In fact the notebooks reveal that he made a close study of Euclid's *Elements* over a ten year period, and later

ABOVE: A self-portrait of Leonardo da Vinci made around the age of 60: red chalk on paper.

OPPOSITE: In his early forties, around the time he met Luca Pacioli, Leonardo began to take an increasing interest in mathematics, filling many notebooks with geometrical sketches, exercises and calculations. At this time, under the aegis of Pacioli, he also began to study Euclid's *Elements*, dedicating around a hundred pages of notes on this subject. Leonardo, who had described himself as 'unlettered', earnestly wanted to improve his knowledge of formal geometry, and even learned basic Latin to facilitate these studies. However, after several years of this he tended to follow his own direction; characteristically, his approach was 'hands-on' and his calculations highly visual rather than abstract.

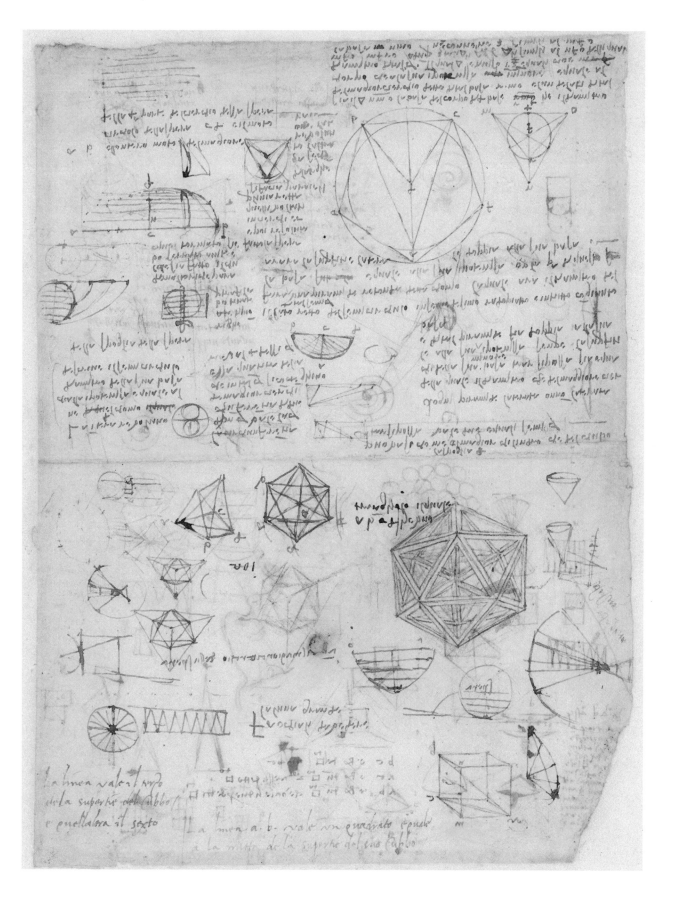

became preoccupied with theories of proportion and various intractable geometrical problems (such as 'Doubling the Cube' and 'Squaring the Circle' - which is in fact impossible). On the more positive side, he made his own proof of Pythagoras' Theorem and produced interesting observations on conical sections and surface areas. Despite his enthusiasm, Leonardo's knowledge of geometry remained fairly basic, but his illustrations for Pacioli's work were rightly described by the author as 'extraordinary and most beautiful figures'. The 'skeletised', or *vacuus*, versions of polyhedra in particular were entirely original and allowed for a more complete, three-dimension visualisation than had previously been possible. On the basis of their accuracy it seems very likely that he made these drawings from actual models of polyhedra, and that he may have used optical aids to draw them, probably including a perspectival window.

It is clear from his fascination with the subject that for Leonardo, as for Pacioli, solid figures had a sublime quality; understanding their forms and the relations between them was to penetrate to the very foundation of reality, and amounted to form of meditation. With Leonardo, as with Pacioli, the vision of Pythagoras and his followers lived on – the universe could best be understood and explained in geometric terms.

*

For Leonardo the optical theory of perspective and the means of achieving it on a plane were bound up with his studies of practical geometry, and both involved the use of the necessary instruments. In painting, as with the other arts and crafts, the eye was deceptive; tools such as the square, compass and measuring rods were essential to penetrate to the divine reality behind illusory appearances. In the same spirit, the polyhedra that so fascinated him were not simply objects to exercise his drawing skills, they were, in the full Platonic sense, the building blocks of reality. But he was also clearly fascinated with the physical objectivity of geometric objects. They could be measured, their transformations from one to the other, and their relative volumes, could be plotted; they offered a deep and direct experience of Nature.

Leonardo's notebooks are littered with geometrical figures, as if he was constantly visualising and turning them over in his mind. The drawings of his attempts at 'Squaring the Circle', which are preserved in one of the notebooks held in the Royal Collection, indicate the extent of his restless, imaginative approach to mathematical problems. The sheet is entirely covered in small geometric sketches and notes – and there are many others of this kind; one contains no less than ninety-three drawings of what he describes as his *Ludo Geometrica* (geometric game). In 1515 he prepared hundreds of quadrature problems for this book, which was probably based on Alberti's *Ludi Geometrico* and Nicholas of Cusa's *De Ludo Globi*, both of which have a rather more 'metaphysical' aspect than a conventional parlour-game.

In another notebook he writes a short passage indicating the seriousness of his commitment to the subject, containing the solemn phrase – 'Let no one who is not a mathematician read my principles'

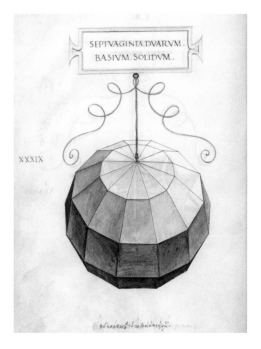

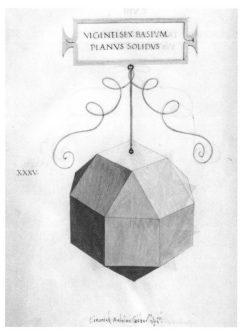

LEFT: These drawings of polyhedra were originally made for Luca Pacioli's *De Divina Proportione* to illustrate his exposition on the Divine (or Golden) ratio. With the addition of labels and ribbons they were later presented as full-page illustrations. The ribbons, which were a conventional way of presenting suspended scientific objects at the time of the Renaissance, were intended to convey a greater sense of solidity and realism – and in so doing, to emphasise the principles of perspective in depicting three-dimensionality.

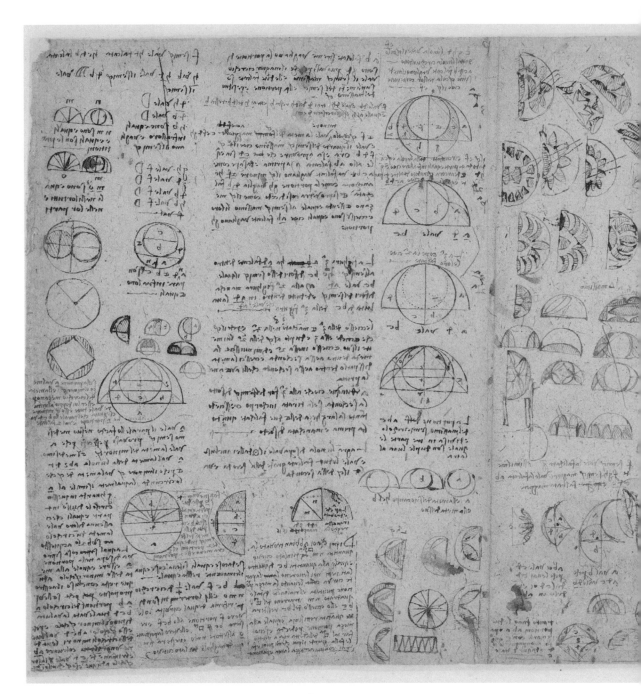

ABOVE: There are many pages of drawings of *Lunulae*, overlapping arcs of a circle, in Leonardo's notebooks. He used these for various geometrical purposes – to calculate square roots, and in his attempts to solve area measurement problems (including the squaring the circle). Leonardo's pursuit of this last problem actually took up a disproportionate amount of his time in later years and is the principle subject of his uncompleted treatise *De Ludo Geometrico* ('The Geometric Game').

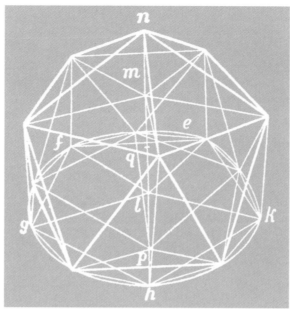

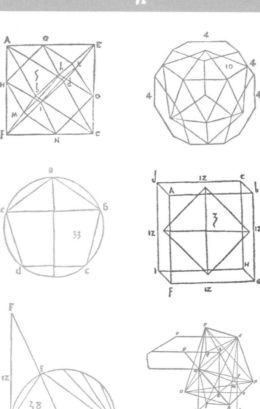

LEFT: Together with the many drawings of polyhedra in *De Divina Proportione*, fifty-nine in all, Leonardo presented a great number of analytical diagrams of the three-dimensional geometrical figures presented in the book, presumably under the direction of Luca Pacioli. It was during the time that they worked together on this project that Leonardo acquired an enthusiasm for geometry that was sustained for the rest of his life. Mathematics and Geometry were important to this man, whose curiosity seemed boundless. He felt, in true Platonic/ Pythagorean fashion, that all natural phenomena are governed by mathematical rules, and that all structures, natural and man-made, are ruled by geometrical proportions–

HARMONIC PROPORTION IN THE HUMAN FIGURE

The notion that the ideal human body should conform to a canon of proportion, which was revived and developed during the Renaissance by Luca Pacioli, Leonardo da Vinci and Albrecht Dürer among others, had its roots in the Classical past. It is another example of the revival of Classical (and particularly Platonic) thought that was initiated at Marsilio Ficino's New Academy in Florence. In Platonic terms, the spirit of rational enquiry should suffuse all areas of erudition and skill, both intellectual and aesthetic; following the dictate that 'That which puts its trust in measurement is the best part of the soul'. It was as important, therefore, to uncover the correct laws of proportion for the representation of the human body, as it was to find the ideal proportions in architecture.

There were, it would seem, Ancient Egyptian precedents for the systemisation of human proportions, but the earliest example in the European tradition is that of the Greek sculptor Polykleitos (5th – early 4th centuries BC). The Polykleitian canon held that a statue of the ideal human form (and of course, the human form itself) should express a series of ideal proportions. It is not entirely certain what Polykleitos had in mind, but it is most likely that it would have been the Pythagorean

intervals, i.e. the octave 1:2; the harmonic fifth 2:3; and the harmonic fourth 3:4.

The Roman architect Vitruvius (see left and spread 29) inherited these Greek ideas of ideal proportions, and incorporated the notion that the human figure should be the ultimate source of proportionality into his own, modular, architectural schemes.

The Renaissance artists mentioned above developed their own analyses and canons of the human figure, but these were naturally greatly influenced by their understanding of Classical precedents.

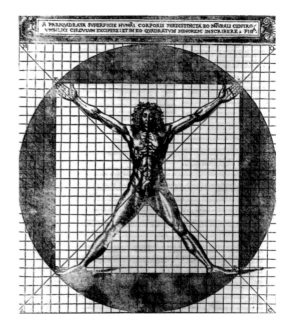

VITRUVIAN MAN

Leonardo's famous drawing is based on the precepts of the canon of proportion governing the human body that were laid out by the Roman Architect Vitruvius, in Book III of his famous and influential treatise *De Architectura*.

'For the human body is so designed by nature that the face, from the chin to the top of the forehead and the lowest roots of the hair, is a tenth part of the whole height; the open hand from the wrist to the tip of the middle finger is just the same; the head from the chin to the crown is an eighth, and with the neck and the shoulder from the top of the breast to the lowest roots of the hair is a sixth; from the middle of the breast to the summit of the crown is a fourth. If we take the height of the face itself, the distance from the bottom of the chin to the underside of the nostrils is one third of it; the nose from the underside of the nostrils to a line between the eyebrows is the same; from there to the lowest roots of the hair is also a third, comprising the forehead. The length of the foot is one sixth the height of the body; of the forearm, one fourth; and the breadth of the breast is also one fourth.'

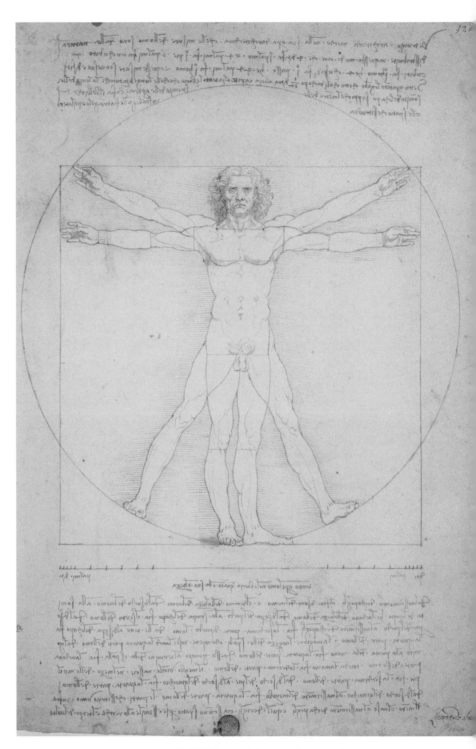

OPPOSITE PAGE: – Ideal proportions; from Cesare Cesariano's edition of Vitruvius's *De Architectura*.

ABOVE: Leonardo's iconic drawing of *Vitruvian Man*: circa 1490, inspired by the Roman architect Marcus Vitruvius Pollio.

MICROCOSMIC MAN

Vitruvian theories of the universality of human proportions were taken up in the earlier Renaissance by many of the more occult-minded magician/scientists (such as Heinrich Agrippa, Paracelsus, Giordano Bruno and Robert Fludd: see spr.no. 85), who attached it to mystical ideas concerning Man's place in the Universe.

These notions, originating with Marsilio's translations of the *Corpus Hermetica*, saw the Cosmos as a Macrocosm which had a mystical, and complete, association with Man, the Microcosm. In this way the Vitruvian concept of 'Man as the measure of the Universe' was divinely (or magically) extended – so that Man, uniquely in the Creation, 'could enjoy the honour of participating in everything': Agrippa, *De Occulta Philosophia*. Man – and these ideas tended to concentrate on the masculine representatives of the species – 'is the most beautiful and harmonic work of God, and contains all the numbers, measures, weights, movements, elements and everything'. Correspondences could be found between the human body, the signs of the Zodiac, celestial bodies – and much else.

As in most of this European occult tradition there are a great many interpretations of this broad theme, varying from author to author. But the idea was compelling enough for it to be taken into the later occult systems of Freemasonry and Rosicrucianism.

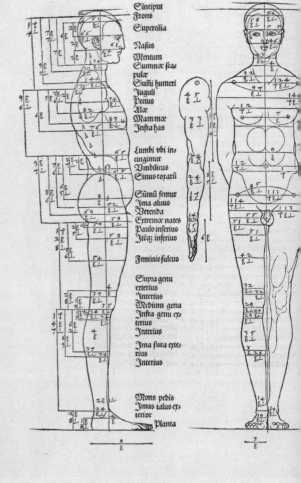

RIGHT: From Heinrich Cornelius Agrippa's *Of Occult Philosophy* published in Basel in 1510.

FAR RIGHT: From the edition of Vitruvius's *De Architectura*, published in Italy in 1521 by Cesare Cesariano.

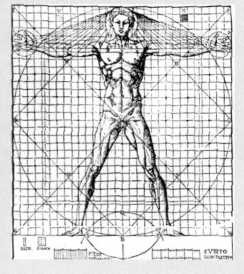

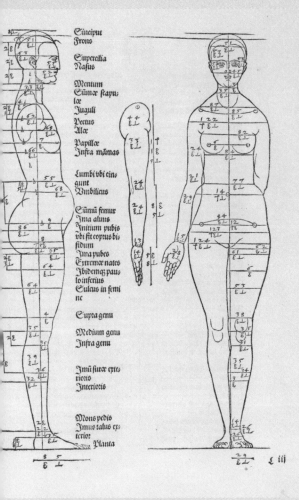

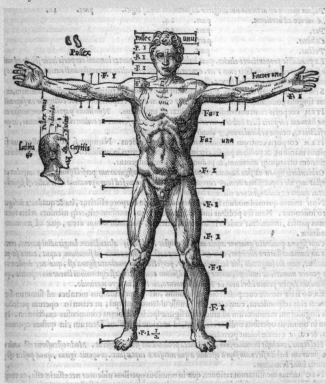

ABOVE: From the patrician humanist Daniele Barbaro's *Della Perspettiva*. Barbaro made his own translation of Vitruvius's *Ten Books on Architecture*.

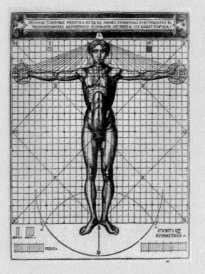

LEFT: This is also from Cesare Cesariano's edition of Vitruvius.

GEOMETRY & PROPORTION
IN THE SHAPING OF LETTERS

In lettering, as in so many other areas, the Humanists of the Renaissance rejected their medieval inheritance and looked to the Classical past for stylistic models. The inscriptional capitals on long-abandoned Roman buildings were their main source of inspiration. Roman stone lettering, with its fine sense of balance and proportion, was founded on geometric principles, which the Renaissance calligraphers attempted to understand and emulate in reconstructing their scripts.

The leading figure in this revival was Felice Feliciano (1433–1479) a self-taught antiquarian and epigrapher who dedicated his life to uncovering and deciphering inscriptions throughout Roman Italy. Feliciano understood the underlying geometric basis of Roman lettering and made his own interpretation of their construction in his *Alphabetum Romanum* of 1460. For Feliciano the Roman letters were formed using a canon derived from Vitruvius (*q.v.*) that was based on combinations of the circle within a square grid. The ratio between the height and width of the letters was 1:10, the 'perfect' proportion of Pythagoras.

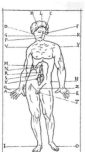
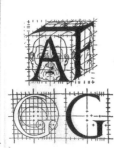

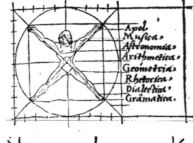

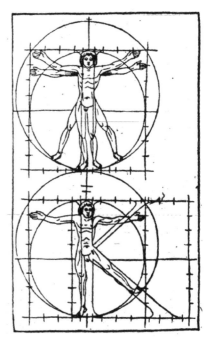

ABOVE AND RIGHT: Geoffroy Tory, a Parisian typographer, emphasised the connection between the proportions in letters and the proportions of the human body in his theoretical work *Champfleury* (1529). This inventive, pioneering typographer also introduced accents, the apostrophe and the cedilla into European typography.

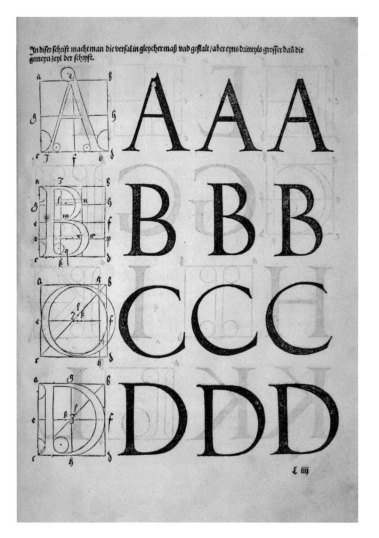

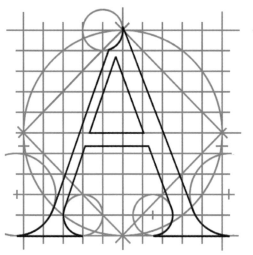

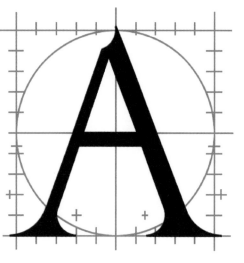

LEFT: A page from Albrecht Dürer's master-work on lettering *On the Just Shaping of Letters* from his *Unterweysung der Messung* ('Instructions on Measurement').

LEFT: From Geoffroy Tory's *Champfleury* in which he lays out his theory on the design of Roman capitals.

Feliciano lived long enough to be able to see his work published in the revolutionary new process of printing (in 1576). But others were also making contributions in this field, notably Luca Pacioli in *De Divina Proportione*, the first printed book to deal with letter construction (in which he may have been assisted by Leonardo da Vinci) and Sigismondo Fanti. Fanti, a mathematician from Ferrara, published two books on penmanship, in which he stresses the role of geometry in the construction of letters. Like Feliciano, he used the circle and the square as building blocks, but tended to extend his letterforms beyond the strict limits of these proportional lines.

Francesco Torniello (1490–1589), who was a mathematician and Franciscan friar like Pacioli, was determined to further improve the new Roman script for the new requirements of movable type. Naturally, in common with all other Renaissance typographers, he used regular geometry, in his case a square, eighteen by eighteen, grid.

In his *Unterweysung der Messung* ('Instructions on Measurement', 1525), Albrecht Dürer deals with the proper forming of the Latin alphabet, providing very precise instructions. Each letter is based on a square, and he specifies that the letters line-widths should be within one thirtieth to one tenth of the square. Serifs are derived from arcs that are also a regular fraction of the underlying square. His lettering system had the elegance one would expect from such a great master and made an enormously influential contribution to European type-design – it is perhaps overcritical to point out, as some typographers have, that he occasionally fudged his own instructions to get the perfect result.

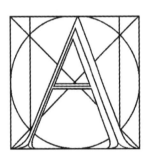

ABOVE: Felice Feliciano, Verona, 1460.

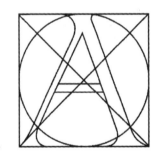

ABOVE: Hartmann Schedel, Munich, 1482.

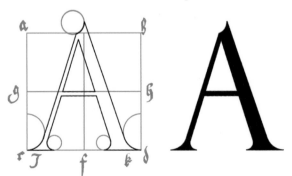

ABOVE: Albrecht Dürer, Nuremberg, 1525.

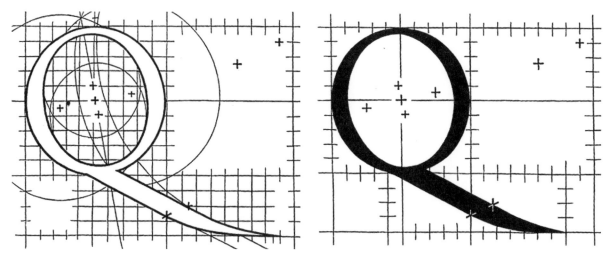

ABOVE: The intricate construction of Geoffroy Tory's capitals in his *Champfleury*, 1529

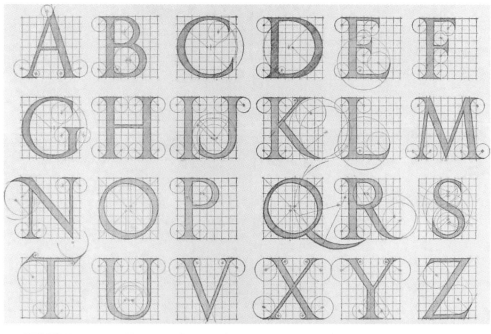

LEFT: A modern version of Dürer's of capital letters adapted and reconstructed by F.C. Brown.

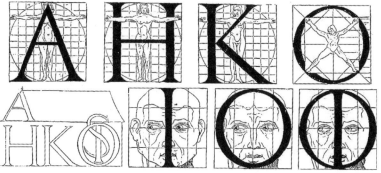

LEFT: In his *Champfleury* Tory manages to combine his grid-based system of lettering with a preoccupation with human proportions and physiognomy.

IDEAL CITIES OF THE RENAISSANCE

There was a vogue, which endured through all the years of the Renaissance, for the conceptualisation of an Ideal City. There were various motivations behind these utopian-inspired endeavours – to create more congenial living spaces, to inspire citizenship, to improve the moral climate and,

ABOVE: The fortified city of Milan in the 16th century, from the *Mappa di Antonio Lafreri.*

not least, to consolidate local rule. Above all, the Ideal City, in contrast to existing medieval towns, would be *planned*. Some theorists were concerned with a reformation of the social structure of cities, but for the majority the emphasis was on the *physical* arrangement of the *Città Ideale* – the majority of which assumed that the ideal city-plan would be based on a simple geometrical, preferably polygonal, arrangement This was in part a desire to recreate the regular grid formations of Roman towns, but was also a reflection of the Platonic association between Ideal Forms and Geometry. Many of the prominent figures of the Italian Renaissance, artists, sculptors and philosophers as well as architects, contributed to this

debate – including Leon Battista Alberti, Leonardo Da Vinci and Albrecht Dürer among others.

As with so many of the intellectual movements of the Renaissance, much of the inspiration for these ideas was drawn from the Classical past. Two sources were of particular importance in this regard, namely, Plato's *Republic* (which is itself a prescription for an ideal society), and Vitruvius's *De Architectura* (the first part of which is dedicated to town-planning). Latterly, a distinctly Utopian flavour was added to these speculations, sparked off by the publication of Sir Thomas More's *Utopia* in 1516 (see box). This book generated a great deal of interest in Humanist circles throughout Europe and gave rise to an outpouring of utopian literature. *

Alberti, whose book on perspective *De Pictura* had exerted a profound influence on Renaissance artists, joined this debate with another classic treatise, *De Re Aedificatoria* ('On the Art of Building').** This volume of ten-books was very much based on

MORE'S *UTOPIA*

Sir Thomas More's *Utopia* (Greek for *No-Land*) was first published in Latin in 1516. It is a remarkable work, not least because More's intentions in writing it, and his attitude to the egalitarian society that he portrays, are far from clear. His Utopia (a term that he devised) is communistic to the point of tedium. All the towns in his vision are built on the same uniform plan; all the inhabitants speak the same language, are governed by the same laws and have the same customs and institutions. On the material level, wealth is shared by all. The cities in this realm are geometric in plan and surrounded by a wall. The citizens, by contrast with those in existing European countries, are entirely rational in their behaviour, religiously tolerant and possessed

ABOVE: *Sir Thomas More* by Hans Holbien.

of high ethical standards. The manners of the town's inhabitants are thus reflective of the town's orderly civic arrangements.

More's ideas in *Utopia* are clearly drawn from Plato, especially *The Republic*, but also from *De Architectura*

by the Roman architect Vitruvius. However, these and other sources are thoroughly re-interpreted in accordance with his Christian-Humanist outlook. Although his was not the first book to lay out ideas for a more equable society, More's proposals created a great deal of interest and inspired many others to create their own versions of perfect towns and perfect societies, particularly in Italy (where it was translated in 1548). It also established an enduring literary form, Utopian-fiction.

Ironically, *Utopia* was not published in England until 1551, sixteen years after Sir Thomas More's execution for treason, on the orders of Henry the Eighth.

Vitruvius, but quotes from a number of Classical authors. On the practical side, Alberti deals with the types and uses of different materials, describes methods of construction, and dedicates four of his books to the appropriate ornamentation of buildings according to their civic function. He also presents his own aesthetic vision of building and town-planning, declaring that 'the harmony of all parts' was dependent on special arrangements of number and proportion. Alberti uses the circle and square as his ideal forms, particularly for the ground-plans of sacred buildings, and he associates regular polygons and rectangles derived from these with musical harmonies. There is a clear link here to Pythagorean

principles, which of course he would also have encountered in Vitruvius.

Some twenty years after Alberti's book another appeared that addressed the same concerns. This also drew on Vitruvius, and was equally preoccupied with Pythagorean number-mysticism, but Filarete's *Trattato di Architettura* is a very different production. 'Filarete' (Antonio di Pietro Averlino) uses the Classical form of a dialogue – the book is presented in the form of an extended dissertation (between an architect and his patron) that manages to weave pragmatic technical advice on the construction of buildings with fantastical speculations about the magical potency of geometry and the importance of astrological reckoning. Filarete makes elaborate categories of buildings according to their age and function and, in common with Vitruvius, he scales his buildings using the human figure, taking the head as the basic architectural unit. As with other schemes of this kind there is an interaction between aesthetic and ethical/moral considerations. Filarete constantly stresses the need to maintain celestial harmony The primary focus of his book though is on a proposed new city, Sforzinda, commissioned by his patron the *condottiero* Francesco Sforza, the Duke of Milan (see box).

Francesco di Giorgio Martini's *Trattato di Architettura* was a far more down-to-earth contribution to this literary form. An exhaustive, fully illustrated treatise on architectural practice that was compiled throughout his twenty-year career, it was intended as a working manual for aspiring architects. It was highly original at the time of its publication in 1482 since a comprehensive reference work of this sort was unavailable. Francesco di Giorgio was disparaging about Alberti's architectural treatise and clearly intended to produce a volume that he saw as more genuinely useful – which it was, with the sheer quantity of its theoretical and practical advice, to architects and builders alike. Many of his innovations in building practice were adopted and became part of the architectural repertoire – but the third part of his compendium is largely concerned with his notions of an Ideal City which were illustrated, as had become the custom, with detailed geometric ground-plans. Francesco di Giorgio was very much of his time in identifying the ground plans of churches, and of his city-plans, with the shape of the human figure. In this anthropomorphic equation Man, as the creation of God, represented divine

RENAISSANCE UTOPIAN VISIONS

These imaginary cityscapes, all of which date from the second half of the 16th century, can be seen as a perfect expression of various interconnected preoccupations of that time. The Renaissance was, above all else, a time of renewal; new ideas were appearing not only in the ways that painting and architecture could be done, but also in technology, in social organisation and philosophy. The utopian visions of ideal urban landscapes shown here reflect these aspirations, which included a nostalgia for the geometric formalism of Classical architecture. The dream-like sense of space and brightness in these images (and the absence of those annoying intrusions, people) portray an idealised view of the City that was in clear contrast with the jostling, squalid realities of the medieval towns with which most were familiar. This is the stage-set of a Humanist utopian paradise, reflecting their ambitions of a complete reformation of manners and culture.

There are, however, uncertainties about the provenance and precise artistic intention of these paintings – and indeed, their original titles. The medium is tempera and the theme and style of the painting are very similar; if not by the same hand, the artists are likely to have been in contact. It is possible that all of the paintings were commissioned by Duke Federico da Montefeltro of Urbino, who would certainly have been sympathetic to their *Ideal City* theme. The upper version has been variously attributed to Piero Della Francesca, Leon Battista Alberti, Luciano Laurana and Francisco di Giorgio Martini – four very distinct artistic personalities. The middle painting, also known as the *Ideal City*, is usually associated with Fra Carnevale, but others see Martini's hand in this work. The lower version is a panel that was originally intended to decorate a *cassone* (a chest for clothes or linen), and may also have been the work of Francisco di Giorgio. None of these attributions are entirely reliable, but it is clear that whoever was responsible had completely mastered the recently developed techniques of perspective.

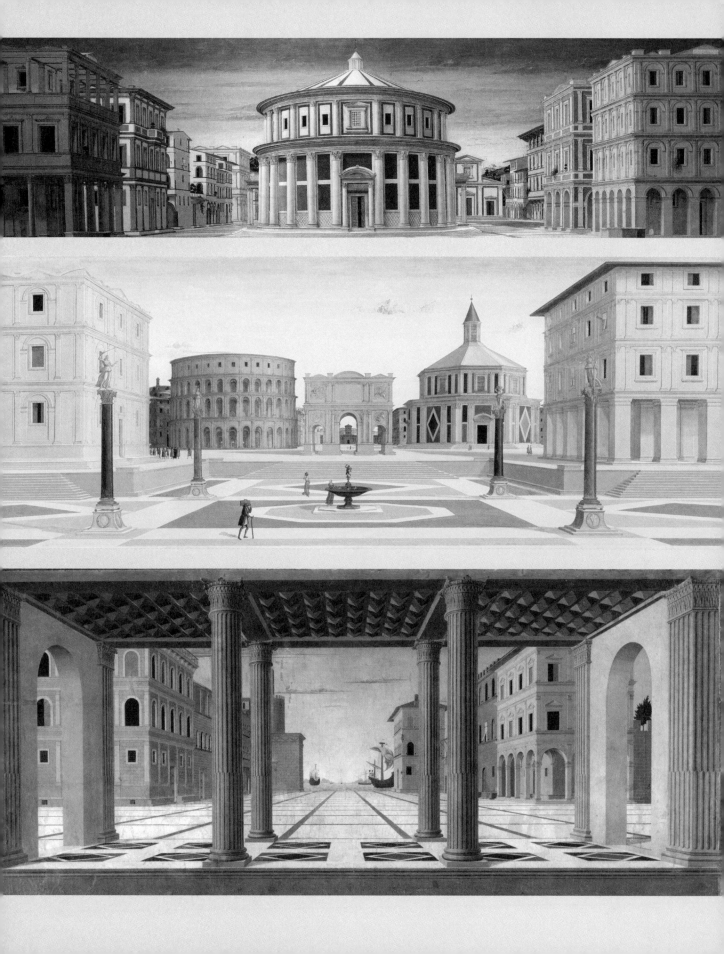

perfection; human form and symmetry became the basis of architectural form and symmetry.

*

From the beginning, the Italian Renaissance *Città Ideale* was conceived as a fortified city - hardly surprising in view of the continuous threat of warfare during this period. But in the course of the 16th century the notions of an Ideal City and the requirements for new defendable towns became increasingly intertwined; fashion was also implicated in this. By the middle of the century many of the features of earlier theories, together with the latest ideas on fortification, were both being incorporated into newly created and older adapted towns. Thus it was that Star Forts, of one kind or another, were built right across Europe to

STAR FORTS

Star-shaped fortifications, or *Trace Italienne*, which were originally introduced as a measure to deal with the increasing use of cannon in siege warfare, developed in parallel, and had a continuing in-teraction with Renaissance notions of the Ideal City. In Italy in particu-lar, the deployment of extended battlements to provide covering fire became a logistical necessity to deal with the more modern cannon used by the French invaders of the Peninsula. These arrangements did away with 'dead-zones', preventing the enemy from getting too close to the city walls. Other aspects of military defence, such as complex, defendable street-grids, also fed into ideas of town-planning from the mid 16th century on.

The problems of fortification attracted the attention of many theorists and practitioners in Italy at this time, (including Michelangelo, who helped re-design Florence's defences), and the proposed solutions were a

Plans of Star Forts from Jacques Ferret's *Fortifications et Artifices, Architecture et Perspective*

prominent feature in most of the notions of Ideal Cities that were put forward. By the middle of the 16th century the defensive schemes advocated by Italian architects and military theorists, particularly the Star Fort, were taken up throughout Europe, where the form persisted until the invention of the explosive shell in the 19th century, a development that rendered such fortifications obsolete.

consolidate borders; in France by Francois I, in the Spanish Netherlands, by the Venetians in Cyprus and by Rudolph II on the Hapsburg borders with the Ottoman Turks. There were occasional conflicts between the ideals of architectural geometricism and the brute requirements of military contingency, but the continuing use of the polygonal-star schema remained extraordinarily persistent.

* Including Tommaso De Campella's *City of the Sun*, and Bartholomeo Del Bene's *City of Truth*.
** Alberti's work became the first printed book on Architecture (in 1485) and was closely followed by the first printed version of Vitruvius (in 1486).

SFORZINDA & PALMANOVA

The first detailed plan for an 'Ideal City' in the Renaissance was produced by the Florentine architect Filarete (Antonio di Pietro Averlino) in his *Trattato di Architettura*, 1465. **Sforzinda** was named after Francesco Sforza, the Duke of Milan and founder of the Sforza dynasty. In the event it was never built, but it represented the most meticulous piece of town-planning that had ever been seen up to that time. Sforzinda was laid out on a star-pattern based on two squares at 45°, which enclosed a concentric street-plan. There were to be towers at the outer points of the star and gates at the inner corners, to which the town's avenues radiated from a large central square. This arrangement included an elaborate system of interconnecting canals which were to be linked to a river to facilitate the distribution of goods of all kinds, inwards and outwards. Although never realised, Filarete's schema was very influential on other planned cities including some that were actually built. It became a sort of prototype of the Utopian Renaissance City, giving rise to a host of other versions, the most notable being **Palmanova**.

Palmanova was founded by the Venetian Republic in celebration of its victory over the Turkish Ottomans at the Battle of Lepanto, and as a defence against any further incursions from that quarter. Sforzinda was taken as the primary source of inspiration for this new, fortified town. Like Sforzina, Palmanova was conceived

ABOVE: The fortified city of *Palmanova*: the most complete realisation of the Renaissance Ideal City. This project was overseen by the aristocratic patrician Mercantonio Barbaro, brother of the Humanist Daniele Barbaro.

as a concentric city, based on a star-plan, with a series of ring-roads that intersected radial avenues. The architect responsible, Giulio Savorgnano, proposed that every citizen would have equal access to land and facilities (echoes of More's *Utopia* perhaps), and it was expected that the harmonious geometry of the city would promote a sense of well-being and culture. Unfortunately, this was not to be. The Venetians, it turned out, were extremely reluctant to leave their watery confines for what was essentially a garrison town on an uncertain border.

ANDREA PALLADIO &
HARMONIC PROPORTIONS

The Humanist project to revive the culture of Antiquity naturally had a powerful influence on architecture during the Renaissance. A leading figure in this movement, and indeed one of the most influential figures in the history of European architecture, was Andrea Palladio (1508–1580).

Palladio was born in Padua, in modest circumstances, as Andrea di Pietro. His extraordinary career begun when he went to work with local stonemasons, but at the age of 16 he moved to nearby Vicenza, where he joined the Guild of stonecutters and masons. His talent was noticed whilst working on the villa of the Humanist scholar and author Gian Giorgio Trissino. Trissino was the leading intellectual of the Venetian Republic at this time, with wide-ranging interests that included literature, science, medicine and botany. He became a teacher and mentor to the young Andrea and chose to educate him in the Classics. Such was his pupil's receptivity to this knowledge that he renamed him Palladio, after *Pallas Athene*, the Greek Goddess of Wisdom.

ABOVE: Andrea Palladio 1508–1580

Palladio soon came to share Trissino's passion for Roman architecture, and for the work of the Roman architect Vitruvius (see side bar) – and such was their shared enthusiasm for this subject that they made trips to Rome to draw and measure its surviving monuments. These expeditions, together with Vitruvius's book *De Architectura*, which Trissino also introduced him to, made a deep impression on Palladio and inspired his own development as an architect. As well as acquiring a Classical education at Trissino's Villa, Palladio befriended many of the younger aristocracy of Vicenza – several of whom went on to become his patrons.

Palladio was eventually responsible for some forty villas around Vicenza alone – and the style he developed came to exert an enormous influence on Western architecture. His designs were marked by simple, strong symmetries, with rooms arranged

OPPOSITE TOP LEFT AND BOTTOM: Plans, elevations and sectional views of Palladio's architecture.
TOP RIGHT: Palladio's drawing of the *Pantheon* in Rome: from his magnum opus *Quattro Libri dell'Architettura* ('The Four Books of Architecture'), published in Venice in 1570.

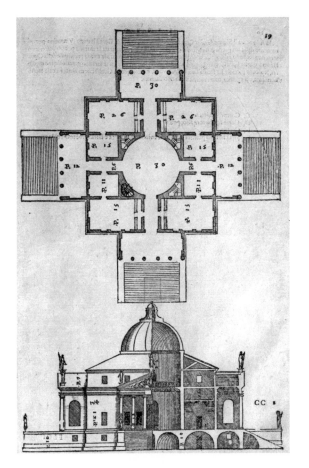

according to harmonic mathematical ratios. In addition, Palladio audaciously adopted the form of Greek pediments and columns from Classical Temples for the façades of the private residences of his Vicenza clients. After some twenty years as a successful working architect Palladio published *I Quattro Libri dell' Architectura* ('Four Books of Architecture'; 1570), a publication that was obviously inspired by Vitruvius's *De Architectura*. This contained several of Palladio's drawings of reconstructions of Roman buildings, but was primarily concerned to present his own architectural theories – which were very influential. It was gradually accepted throughout Europe and was particularly successful in Britain. In essence, Palladianism, as his style became known, was an advance on Renaissance Classicism, nevertheless his outlook was completely imbued with the Platonism that he had learned from Trissino. The original source of this movement, of course, were the concepts developed in Marsilio Ficino's Florentine Academy; harmonic proportionality was the key to

Beauty - in architecture, as in art and music.

*

Vitruvius's *De Architectura* had been rediscovered in 1414 and, as the only architectural treatise to have survived from the Classical period, it became an important source of inspiration for all Renaissance architects concerned with the Classical revival. From the time that he was introduced to this work Palladio was sympathetic to the principles of proportion and symmetry that it extolled – namely, the harmonic proportions that the author described as having been revealed by Pythagoras and Plato. Palladio was also entirely sympathetic with the Vitruvian notion that buildings should reflect the supposed ideal proportions of the human body, the ratios of which were produced by the Divine Will. The underlying supposition here was that buildings should participate and reflect the harmony of the cosmic order.

Palladio made his own interpretation of Pythagorean harmonics and developed a set of general rules of architectural proportion. He adopted

PALLADIO & CARDINALE DANIELE BARBARO

When his friend and patron Gian Giorgio Trissino died Palladio found new supporters in the powerful Barbaro brothers, Daniele and Marcantonio. Daniele Barbaro was himself a prominent Humanist intellectual and patron of the arts and sciences. He encouraged Palladio in his enthusiasm for Classical architecture, and accompanied him on further visits to Rome. Through the influence of the Barbaros Palladio gained entrée to the patrician circles of Venice, where he eventually became the Chief Architect of the Venetian Republic.

Daniele Barbaro was a complex, multi-talented individual in his own right. He was the author of several

books on a wide range of topics, including Philosophy, Mathematics and Astronomy – remarkably, he too was an Architect. In 1567 Barbaro published a *Commentario* on Vitruvius's *De Architectura* (which included drawings by Palladio), in a work that is regarded as the culmination of Renaissance efforts to come to grips with its theoretical content. At the time Barbaro's commentary was an important contribution to the debate on aesthetics in general, and it is interesting that he acknowledges Palladio's expertise, both architectural and archaeological, in his interpretation of this subject.

the Vitruvian recommendation of fixed moduli and proposed seven distinct ratios for the shapes of rooms, and three different ratios for height to width – all of which conform to the regular Pythagorean ratios 3:4, 2:3, 3:5 etc. (the only exception being √2:1). Palladio's 'symphonic' principles of architectural proportion, with their association of musical with spatial values, were completely in accord with Humanist ambitions to revive the grandeur and elegance of the Classical past.

VITRUVIUS & *DE ARCHITECTURA*

Marcus Vitruvius Pollio, known simply as Vitruvius, wrote his masterpiece *De Architectura* in Rome around 15 BCE, at the time of the Emperor Augustus. This positively encyclopaedic work dealt with every aspect of Roman architecture, urban planning and civil engineering. It consists of ten Books dedicated to such specific subjects as the choice of site, the appropriate materials for particular buildings, working methods and the training of architects. Vitruvius had extensive personal experience in these fields, but also seems to have drawn on the earlier writings of Greek and Etruscan architects.

Of particular interest here is the section in which Vitruvius lays out his observations on architectural aesthetics (in Chapter 2 of Book 1) – ideas that clearly had a wide currency at the time of writing. According to these, the architectural canon derives from four interdependent categories – *ordinatio*, *dispositio*, *eurythmia* and *symmetria* (all of which terms are Greek in origin). In this context *symmetria* means that the measurements of the different parts of a building should be in regular proportion with each other; to express the beauty of order. *Eurythmia* is concerned with the placement of the various elements of a building, the beauty of disposition. *Ordinatio* and *dispositio* are the means of achieving these values. Vitruvius is at pains to explain that architectural harmony rises from both the details of a building and the ways in which these correspond to the form of the design as a whole. The human body, with its proportionate cubit, foot, palm and inch, is used throughout his writing as a model for *eurythmy*. In the Renaissance, with the rediscovery of *De Architectura*, this latter notion (variously interpreted it has to be said), became a universally accepted architectural axiom.

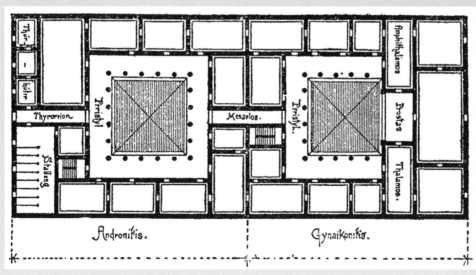

LEFT: A plan of a Greek house from Vitruvius's *De Architectura*.

GEOMETRIA & THE LIBERAL ARTS

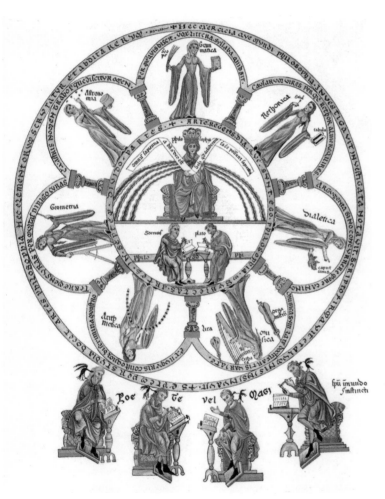

ABOVE: 'Philosophy and the Seven Liberal Arts', from the 12th century manuscript *Hortus Delicarum* which drew on Classical and Islamic sources. The Liberal Arts were a central part of the basic curriculum in the Late Classical and Roman periods.

The Seven Liberal Arts*, whose origins lay in the Classical world of Greece and Rome, became the formal educational system that was taught for centuries in Medieval Europe. This basic curriculum of academic learning was, in turn, adopted by Renaissance scholars. *Geometria* had always been one of the component subjects of the Liberal Arts – although neither of these terms had quite the same meaning that they have today. The 'Liberal Arts' encompassed a broader range of subjects than the modern 'Arts' (including, as they did, such fields as Maths, Logic and Astronomy); and *Geometria* itself was conceptually more closely tied to its origins as the science of 'Earth-measurement' than the modern notion of Geometry as a branch of pure mathematics.

The 'Liberal Arts' curriculum had in fact been subject to revision at various moments in its long history, most notably in the transition from the Medieval (where it had formed the basis of Scholasticism) to the Renaissance (where it was adjusted to meet the criteria of the new Humanist agenda). The term 'Humanism' (*umanisti*) itself derived from the late medieval *studia humanitatis*,

* Traditionally the Liberal Arts were comprised of the *Trivium* (Grammar, Rhetoric and Logic) and the *Quadrivium* (Music, Arithmetic, Geometry and Astronomy).

the 'studies of humanity', as distinct from the 'studies of the divine'. It represented a shift in moral focus from the purely spiritual to the development of virtue in all its forms, including the civic.

The Humanist version of the Liberal Arts spread rapidly throughout Europe during the 16th century, where it became the basis of new educational requirements not only for ruling elites, as in the past, but for the scions of the increasing (and increasingly aspiring) upper and middle-classes. The advantages of a broad-based education in every aspect of civil life had become obvious, both to Rulers and to those who wanted to find their place in the world. Moreover, the acquisition of knowledge had become fashionable.

The depiction of the Seven Liberal Arts as female figures, together with their appropriate attributes, is almost as old as the system itself; the earliest example dates from the 5th century AD. But during the 15th and 16th centuries the new invention of printing allowed series of engravings depicting this theme to became very popular. In these versions *Geometria* is frequently portrayed beside a Globe, accompanied by the instruments of her calling (rules, dividers, squares etc.). The prints often also include the chief representatives of the particular Liberal Art that is being portrayed, usually an important personage drawn from antiquity. In the case of *Geometria* this is invariably Euclid.

GEOMETRIC MOTIFS IN ITALIAN *INTARSIA*

*I*ntarsia techniques, involving fine wood-inlay work, were part of the rich artistic heritage that came to Europe from the Islamic world via Spain (the term itself may derive from the Arabic *tarsi*, for mosaic or inlay). The Italian city of Siena, in particular, had a long association with the production of fine woodworking, and there are records of panels and doors being decorated in this way from around the mid-15th century. This tradition peaked a half a century later, with some of the finest work produced by such masters as Fra Giovanni da Verona (*c.*1433–1515) and Damiano da Bergamo (*c.*1490–1549), both of whose work clearly shares the preoccupations of fine Artists at this time. Perspective and geometric motifs were common in Italian intarsia panels of the early 16th century, as was the use of *trompe l'oeil* effects. Interestingly, it would seem that Fra Giovanni used tracings of Leonardo's drawings of geometrical figures in some of his panels, where they were clearly regarded as appropriate subjects for religious meditation. The earlier *intarsia* work was exclusively ecclesiastical, but it was soon adopted by (wealthy) Humanist scholars to furnish their own studies – and to provide subjects for their own meditations.

The historian Vasari placed the genre within the realm of painting, and many *intarsistes* relied on painters to provide preparatory drawings for their panels. The medium is particularly suited to geometric themes, and also became completely interwoven with the development of perspective at this time and shared many of its themes. The *intarsia* repertoire frequently presents geometric and liturgical objects, and often shows scientific instruments, together with many portrayals of idealised, enchanted cityscapes. Every object in these panels appears to resonate with symbolic value, much of which seems to reflect the Universal Harmony of Neoplatonism speculation

LEFT: Luca Pacioli's *De Divina Proportione*, with its drawings by Leonardo da Vinci, became a source-book for Fra Giovanni in his *intarsia* panels.

LEFT AND ABOVE: Geometrical figures, scientific instruments and musical instruments frequently appear as motifs in the Intarsia panels of Fra Giovanni da Verona

ABOVE: Intarsia panels by Fra Giovanni da Verona, depicting Astronomy (right) and an idealized version of his home town Verona (left)

ABOVE: Two further Intarsia panels from the monastery Monte Oliveto Maggiore by the master Fra Giovanni da Verona, featuring a Campanus sphere and the tools of intarsia (right), and an idealized view of the ancient city walls of Verona (left)

III

GEOMETRIA
and the
NORTHERN
RENAISSANCE

The great revival of interest in geometry, and the developments in perspective/optics that took place in early Renaissance Italy were duplicated when it moved north of the Alps, and as had been the case in Italy, the stature of those involved in these subjects is an indication of how important they were regarded.

LEFT: The frontispiece of Petrus Apianus' *Instrument Buch*, published in Nuremberg, 1533 was the first printed book on Astronomy and Surveying. The two regular polyhedra are used emblematically as an indication of scientific seriousness

MATHEMATICS, GEOMETRY & PERSPECTIVE NORTH OF THE ALPS

Although civilised life on both sides of the Alps was moved by deep cultural changes during the Renaissance, there were marked contrasts of tone in the ways it affected the major centres. This divergence was, of course, largely attributable to national differences – that is to say, of language, climate and the existing forms of civil society. In Italy, as we have seen, there was a revival of the values of classical antiquity, which inspired a new interest in Latin and Greek. But the most profound effect of Italian humanist ideas on Northern Europe was to act as a catalyst for religious reform, culminating in the upheavals of the Protestant Reformation – one of the consequences of which was a rejection of Latin for scientific, philosophical and intellectual discourse and the adoption of vernacular languages. However, radical influences flowed in both directions; the invention of printing, which originated in Germany, was rapidly taken up in Renaissance Italy, and this innovation greatly facilitated the spread of new ideas wherever it was adopted.

Northern artists travelled to Italy and were deeply impressed by developments there, but again, the stimulus that they received was ultimately more important for its catalytic effect on northern art, rather than as a direct stylistic influence. Renaissance art in the North came to be characterised by a new emphasis on precise observation, realism and naturalism. Typically, when the interest in the regular solids spread to Germany there was rather more emphasis on their practical aspects – how they might be useful in art and how they might explain the physical world. But the philosophical implications of Platonism, the study of the Platonic solids, and the impact of perspective (in all its aspects), were to be as influential here as they had been in Italy.

In Southern Germany there was also a strengthening of the association between the methods of linear perspective and advances in surveying, map-making and astronomy. This was facilitated by the manufacturing traditions (particularly in Nuremberg) that were able to produce the quality of instruments, scientific and otherwise, that were required by these new disciplines. The new industry of printing and publishing, which had also flourished in this area, played an equally important role in this broad movement. Many of the greatest figures of the Northern Renaissance, most of who were notable for the extraordinary range of their accomplishments, were involved in one way or another in these developments.

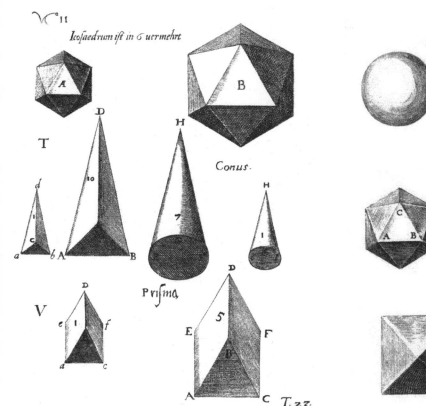

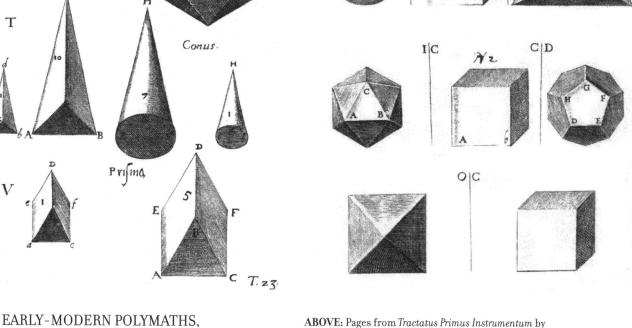

EARLY-MODERN POLYMATHS, PERSPECTIVE AND GEOMETRY

The great revival of interest in geometry, and the developments in perspective/optics that took place in early Renaissance Italy were duplicated when it moved north of the Alps, and as had been the case in Italy, the stature of those involved in these subjects is an indication of how important they were regarded. This period was a time of extraordinary intellectual advances – in science and technology, in geographical exploration, and in astronomical speculation. The Northern Renaissance had its own galaxy of brilliant individuals that made major contributions in these fields, very often across a whole range of disciplines. At this time the towns of southern Germany became the foci of this intellectual ferment and many brilliant scholars

ABOVE: Pages from *Tractatus Primus Instrumentum* by *Mechanicorum* by Hulsius , dealing with solid geometry.

either came from, or chose to live in, such centres as Nuremberg, Augsburg, Ulm and Ingolstadt.

Petrus Apianus (the Latinised version of Peter Bienewitz), 1496–1552, a renowned mathematician and geographer, was one such. Having completed his studies in Leipzig and Vienna he went on to settle in Ingolstadt in Bavaria, where he set up a print shop in 1527. Over the next twenty-five years he published a remarkable series of high quality and much sought after books on such diverse subjects as mathematics, astronomy, geography and cartography. He had an early success with a book on arithmetic that was intended for the practical requirements of trades people and merchants, and written in the vernacular

ABOVE: Petrus Apianus' *Instrument Buch*; The first printed treatise on astronomy and surveying. The frontispiece of this work uses two regular polyhedra, emblematically, as an indication of scientific seriousness.

(interestingly, Apianus's book on Arithmetic is one of the objects shown on the table of Hans Holbein's famous painting *The Ambassadors*).

Other, more luxurious, books on cosmography and astronomy followed; *Cosmographicus Liber*, *Quadrans Apiani Astronomicus*, and the magnificent *Astronomicus Caesareum*, were regarded as masterpieces and went into many editions. He also found time to write an 'Instrument Book' (*Instrument Buch*, 1533) which was the first general treatise on astronomy and surveying. The title-page of this last book is particularly interesting in the present

context as it shows a group using quadrants and other instruments (some of which were devised by Apianus himself), but it also prominently features two polyhedra, a dodecahedron and an icosahedron. His preoccupation with the platonic solids is also indicated in the *Cosmographicus Liber*, where they appear among a charming series of illustrated capitals.

Another distinguished mathematician, Johann Neudorffer (1497–1563), was born in Nuremberg. Like Apianus, he too devised and published tables of commercial arithmetic, and was a teacher of geometry, but achieved his greatest fame as a calligrapher and biographer. Durer employed Neudorffer for the lettering on his 'Apostles' panels, and he was a pioneer typographer, credited with the invention of the *Fraktur* script. Neudorffer is portrayed in a contemporary print as sharing a table with Wenzel Jamnitzer; the two famous sons of the city, geometricians both, are shown with the implements of their trades before them and the town itself looming behind. A caduceus, the symbol of commerce (and of printing) hovers above; an Armillary sphere, symbolic of science and astronomy, stands in the foreground. Johann Neudorffer also appears in a famous portrait by Nicholas Neufchatel in which he is explaining the properties of a dodecahedron to a young pupil.

The extraordinarily talented Levinus Hulsius (1546–1606) was born in Ghent, but moved to Nuremberg in 1583, apparently as a result of his Protestant beliefs. As a linguist he was able to earn a living by teaching languages, but became involved in the manufacture and dealing in geometrical instruments In common with other of the talented individuals mentioned above he

ABOVE: *APIANUS EMBLEMATA*
In his astronomical masterpiece *Cosmographicus Liber*, Petrus
Apianus features a variety of regular geometrical figures as
emblemata in a charming series of illuminated capitals.

ventured into printing and publishing. In 1602 he acquired the printing-plates of Tycho Brahe's *Astronomiae Instauratae Mechanica* and brought out a further edition of that important work. He also wrote a number of treatises on the construction of geometrical instruments, including the *Tractatus Primus Instrumentorum Mechanicorum* 1605, which has a section on geometrical solids. As a lexicographer Hulsius was responsible for compiling and publishing several dictionaries (including French/German and Italian/German). This remarkable man was also active in publishing the most recent accounts of navigations from far-flung parts of the world, together with maps, based on information that he had garnered from sea captains in Antwerp.

LEFT: A detail from the famous portrait of Johann Neudorffer by Nicholas Neufchatel, in which he is explaining the properties of the dodecahedron to a young pupil.

THE 'GEOMETRIC TYPE'

The 'Geometric Type' (*Typus geometriae*), from a popular Encyclopedia, the *Margarita Philosophica*, published by Gegor Reisch in Freiberg in 1503. Dürers biographer Panofsky says of this print 'Geometry, depicted as a richly attired lady is engaged in measuring a sphere with her compass, she sits at a table on which there are drafting implements and models of stereometric bodies'. Her assistants perform various tasks that involve geometrical skills — including astronomy, surveying, building and mechanical handling. The *Margarita* was a widely used textbook that attempted to contain all human knowledge; it is the oldest printed encyclopedia.

PERSPECTIVE GOES NORTH

For a while, the methods of perspective remained the domain of Florence, but they were soon taken up by the other major centres in Italy, and by the early 16th century they had become a standard part of artistic training throughout Europe. Albrecht Dürer encountered the concepts and methods of linear perspective during his first visit to Italy in 1494 and introduced them to other artists on his return to Nuremburg. His enduring fascination with these problems, particularly with the use of perspectival frames, is clear from the number of drawings that he made featuring various versions of this device. Dürer's objectives, and those of other German artists, in using the Albert windows were essentially the same as that of the Italian Renaissance painters. The art of painting and its practitioners would be elevated by placing it on a rigorous, rational basis; only in this way could it become a worthy instrument for the study of nature and, by extension, for revealing the underlying order of the world.

The devices used to attain the required degree of realistic representation, which typically involved reticulated frames, adjustable taut threads and pointers attached to uprights, seem antiquated and over-schematic from the modern viewpoint, but they are an indication of the determination, characteristic of this period, to overcome the deceitful habits of the eye.

RIGHT: A draughtsman is demonstrating a plan of a fortified city to a soldier with the aid of a perspectival frame.

Two plates from Johann Faulhaber's *Newe Geometrische und perspectivische* inventions that indicate the range of his interests.

ABOVE: He is working with a perspectival frame; a book on geometric figures is open on the table; a set of Platonic solids hang from the wall. Through the window on the left we can scenes involving the science of ballistics, of surveying and agriculture. The right-hand window shows an astronomer and an armillary sphere.

ALBRECHT DÜRER:
ARTIST, HUMANIST & GEOMETER

Albrecht Dürer (1471–1528), the most important and influential artist of the Northern Renaissance, was born in Nuremberg, the third child in what was to become a very large family. His father was a goldsmith and expected his son to follow him in this trade, but Dürer's artistic gifts became apparent at a very young age and he was apprenticed to the studio of the painter Michael Wolgemut at the age of fifteen. Such was his prodigious talent that by his mid-twenties he had become a famous and established artist.

Dürer was to make two memorable trips to Italy. The first of these, when he was 23, took him to Venice. The art that he saw, and the artists that he met, made a great impression on him. He returned to Nuremberg brimming with the new ideas of perspective and proportion that he had encountered there, and he became a prime mover in the movement towards a greater accuracy and acuity in representational art that was to sweep across Northern Europe, as it had in Italy.

He made a second Italian trip in 1506–7, again to Venice. But by this time he was more interested in learning about mathematics from Italian sources than in its art. As he had grown older, Dürer had developed a great enthusiasm for geometry. In common with Leonardo, and influenced as the latter

ABOVE: Albrecht Dürer's self-portrait at the age of 28. Painted in 1500, after his first visit to Italy.

was, by Piero della Francesca and Luca Pacioli, Dürer began to argue for a thorough-going, disciplined approach to art – in particular, one that emphasised the role of geometry. He had actually planned to produce a textbook dealing with every aspect of art quite early on in his career, but this never materialised. Towards the end of his life however, in 1525 and 1528, he produced two substantial treatises intended for artists and craftsmen. The first of these, *Underweysung der Messung* ('Instructions in Measurement', Nuremberg, 1525) is of particular interest here.

This was an ambitious textbook in four substantial chapters; it is largely concerned with descriptive geometry, and is accompanied by some 150 illustrations. Written in vernacular German, it was obviously intended for practical rather than theoretical use, although there are frequent references to Euclid. Beginning with the definitions of points, lines and angles it works comprehensively through such matters as conic sections, the construction of polygons and the calculation of areas. It then goes on to the building of architectonic forms, including columns, towers etc. There is also an extended section dedicated to the 'correct shaping of letters', or typography, possibly inspired by similar passages in Pacioli's *De Divina Proportione*. The whole of the final chapter concerns the construction of regular and irregular solids – in which Dürer provides the appropriate plans and instructions to help build these polyhedral forms. Dürer's books on geometry and proportion were, in essence, an attempt to combine the abstract concepts of classical geometry with the traditional geometrical knowledge that had long been practised in the various crafts. His aim seems to have been to put the arts and crafts on

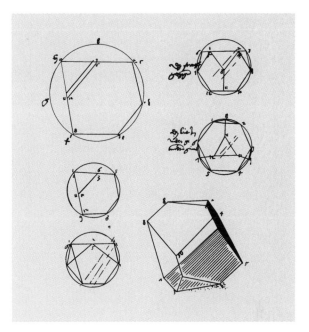

ABOVE: Sketches from one of Dürer's drawing books showing his preliminary ideas for the puzzling irregular polyhedron featured in his famous engraving *Melencolia 1* (see pg. 119).

a sounder, more mathematically-based foundation, and to ennoble them in the process. Interestingly, and as an indicator of its influence at the time, the *Underweysung der Messung* was cited by both Kepler and Galileo in their own published works.

As well as being very influential Dürer's *Underweysung der Messung* and *Vier Bucher von Menschlicher Proportion* ('Four Books on Human Proportion', Nuremberg, 1528) were commercially successful and both were translated and reprinted many times. In fact they became sought-after volumes with an appeal that obviously went far beyond the artist-craftsmen to whom they were ostensibly intended. In effect, Dürer had established a literary genre. After his death many more treatises on geometry and perspective appeared in Germany and elsewhere. Most of these were produced by artist-craftsmen with backgrounds in various trades, practically all of them referred back to Dürer's book on geometry, and most included polyhedra in one form or another.

There was, of course, a financial aspect to the production of these treatises. A new class of bourgeoisie had emerged with money to spend on such prestige items as well produced books and prints. This meant that the emerging medium of printing enabled artists, engravers and woodcutters to make a living at a time when, as a result of the upheavals caused by the Protestant Reformation, art and craft workshops were deprived of income from Church commissions. These artist-craftsmen proved themselves highly adaptable to the new circumstances; the degree of sophistication that was reached in printing techniques, and sheer quantities of print production can be surprising. Dürer's pupil Erhard Schön, for example, is credited with producing over two hundred woodcut prints, and some 1,200 illustrations for 116 books. Schön was exceptionally versatile and prolific, illustrating everything from religious broadsheet propaganda to satirical poetry, but in 1538 he too turned his hand to an artist's manual on design and perspective. There were many other Nuremberg artists that were to take up this idea, and these successors of Dürer, as we shall see, produced a variety of responses to his seminal work.

DÜRER & GEOMETRY

Dürer was the most celebrated artist of the Northern Renaissance and, in common with Leonardo Da Vinci, was thoroughly involved with the Renaissance enthusiasm for science and mathematics, to which he increasingly turned in his later years. In 1525, at the age of 54, he produced a major work on geometry, 'Four Books on Measurement' (*Underweysung der Messung mit dem Zirckel und Richtscheyt*), which examined every aspect of geometrical construction that might be applicable to art and the crafts, including the regular polygons and polyhedra. In the last part of this book Dürer also describes and illustrates various devices for drawing in perspective (*proportionslehre*). This interest in geometry and the sciences was, however, already evident more than a decade earlier, in his famous engraving *Melencholia I* (see p.120).

Dürer's biographer Panofsky was uncertain whether the artist would have been acquainted with Piero della Francesca's geometrical work, or that of Luca Pacioli, but notes that Dürer's approach to the study of polyhedra was in any case rather different. In the *Underweysung* he presents the solids together with the polygonal 'nets' from which they are formed.

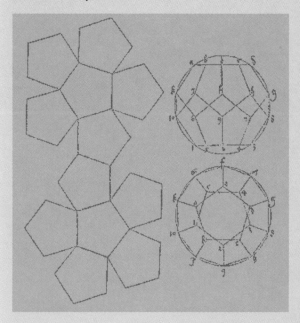

THE MYSTERIES OF *MELENCOLIA I*

This enigmatic and much-debated print, quite apart from its aesthetic intentions, clearly reflects Dürer's interests in science and mathematics. It features a number of architectural instruments and craftsmen's tools, together with an array of allegorical items including a compass, empty scales, a ladder, an hourglass and a magic square. The nature of the solid figure, with its faint trace of a skull, possibly of the artist's mother, has in itself generated a great deal of speculation (it has been seen as a truncated rhombohedron or a partially truncated cube, but actually is neither).

Over the years there have been many conjectures as to the meaning of this print, by very highly regarded scholars. There was little agreement between these interpretations however, and none were entirely convincing. But in 2004, five hundred years after it was created, the British art-historian Patrick Doorly published a comprehensive, and thoroughly plausible, explanation of Dürer's sources and intentions in *Melencholia I*. In essence, Doorly claims, it is based on a text – namely that of Plato's *Greater Hippias*, a Dialogue in which the principle character, Socrates, repeatedly asks 'What is the Beautiful?'. The many objects distributed around the central figure represent the solutions to this question that are grudgingly discounted by Socrates' respondent, the Sophist Hippias. It is reasonable to assume that Dürer knew this Dialogue – it is certain that his great friend and collaborator Willibald Pirckheimer possessed the *Complete Works* of Plato. But there is an additional layer of inspiration for Dürer's print – this is nothing other than Luca Pacioli's *De Divina Proportione*. All of the items featured in *Melencholia* are also traceable to references in this work (with which Dürer was undoubtedly familiar with from his time in Venice), whose text he follows quite literally.

In composing his master-print Dürer converted Pacioli's Platonic explanation and praise of mathematics into an intriguing, playful work of art. In the *Greater Hippias* itself the answer to Socrates' question on the nature of 'the Beautiful' is unanswered; the question is too profound even for Plato. Dürer chose to express this unsatisfactory inconclusiveness with the peevish figure of Melancholy, who belongs to the tradition of the personification of Geometry as a female figure. (see [spr.31a]).

RIGHT: Dürer's famous engraved print of *Melencolia*. This picture is almost over-laden with a range of symbolic imagery that has long puzzled art-historians and has given rise to many different interpretations. A solution has recently been proposed (see left) that links it to Plato's Dialogue *Greater Hippias* – however, Dürer was commercially astute enough to realise that such an intriguing puzzle-piece would have a particular appeal to potential buyers of the print. The significance of the irregular polyhedron, with its faint trace of a skull (possibly of the artist's mother) has in itself generated a great deal of speculation, as has the 'supermagic' square, which has more lines of addition than an ordinary 4×4 magic square, and which manages to show the year of the print's creation, 1514, in the central boxes of the bottom row.

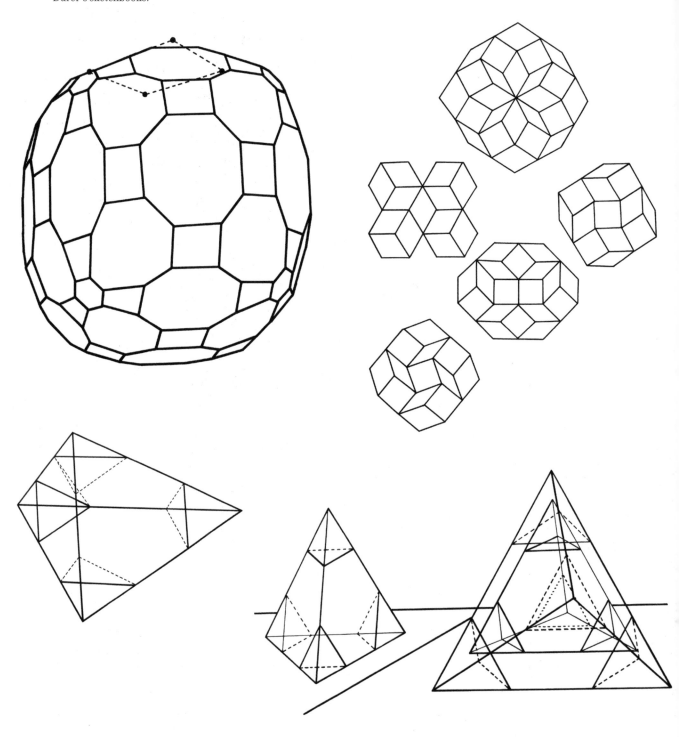

BELOW AND OPPOSITE: Geometrical drawings from
Dürer's sketchbooks.

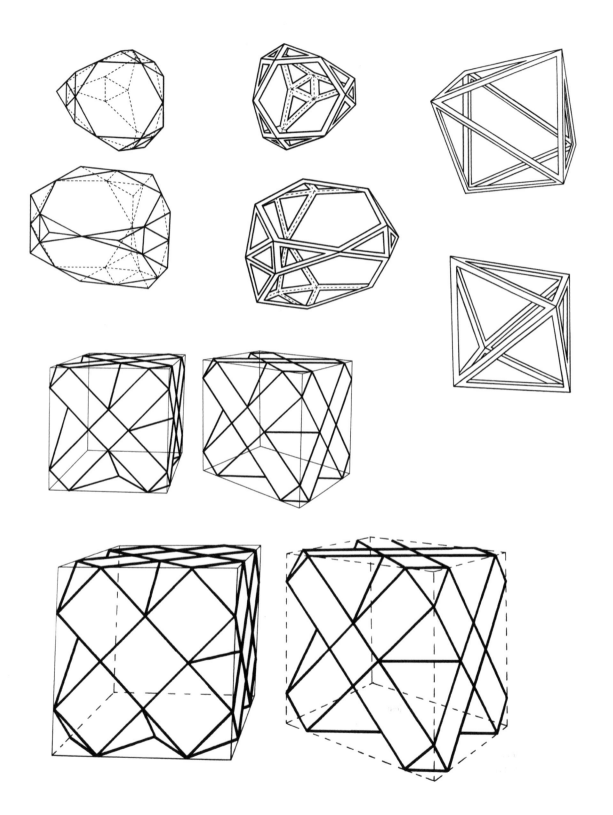

DÜRER'S & LEONARDO'S KNOT PATTERNS

It is an art-historical curiosity that although there is uncertainty whether Dürer ever actually met Leonardo da Vinci while both were in Venice in 1494–5, each artist is associated with a range of prints of elaborate 'knot' designs; six in each series.

TOP: A sketch by Leonardo of an interlacing design, almost certainly of Islamic origin: Codice Atlantico, 701r

ABOVE: A more elaborate interlacing pattern by Leonardo, clearly derived from the above: Codice Atlantico, 700r

These productions are tinged with ambiguities though, not least the fact that Dürer's are exact copies of Leonardo's. Also the degree of Leonardo's involvement in this project is unclear. The most probable explanation is that Dürer came across prints of the designs attributed to 'Leonardo's Studio', perhaps even after his second visit to Venice in 1505, and was inspired to make an edition of his own on his return to Nuremberg. There are suggestions that these prints had a commercial application, as models for embroidery, or possibly for leather book-binding, but this too is conjectural.

Because they fall into the category of an 'applied' art these designs have tended to have been disregarded by fine-art historians, but it is obvious from their elaborate composition that both artists (and/or their collaborators), took the construction of these pieces very seriously. In fact they are masterpieces of intricate knot-design. The immediate source of inspiration probably derived from the Islamic interlace designs found in the ceramics and manuscripts imported from the Middle East, particularly those from Egypt and Syria, with whom Venice had long-standing trade links.

On the basis of many small sketches in his notebooks, and from details of intricate embroidered designs in his paintings, Leonardo was intrigued by interlacing motifs. There is also a marvellously elaborate fresco of interlacing trees attributed to him in the Sala del Asse, in the castle of his patron, Francesco Sforza. However, by contrast with Dürer, Leonardo did not seem at all interested in printing, so his knot designs (and the wood-cuts used to print them) may well have been completed by a member of the 'Leonardo Academia' – whose name is emblazoned on them. The 'Vici' at the centre of these knot patterns could be a pun, referring both to the artist's birthplace and to the Latin term 'to bind'. As an aside, it is interestingly, particularly in light of the fact that Leonardo himself played the lute, that one of the more common openwork designs for the lute rosette of this period is 'the knot of Leonardo'.

The precise involvement of Dürer, and why he chose to copy these prints, is unclear, but the commercial aspect cannot be ignored. It is presumptuous to make a charge of piracy (by one Renaissance Master on another!), but the fact that Dürer removed all of the insignia that referred to Leonardo and his 'Academy' and replaced them in some instances with his own familiar monogram, is rather suspicious. It is, however, certain that his own interest in geometry, in its own right and as it applied to art, was just as strong as Leonardo's; his versions are, if anything, more precise than the originals. This was a fascinating application of geometry to art, and clearly one that both artists felt worthy of their attention.

ABOVE: One of six woodcut versions by Albrecht Dürer of a series of intricate knot designs that originated in Leonardo's 'Academy'

ABOVE: An original engraved print of an intricate knot design, again one of a series of six, from Leonardo's 'Academy'

The intended uses of both of these series are uncertain. They may have been meant as guides for embroidery patterns, or for the fine-tooling of book bindings, or simply as decorative sheets in their own right.

DÜRER'S & LEONARDO'S KNOT PATTERNS

GEOMETRISING THE HUMAN FIGURE

In his *Vier Bücher von Menschlicher Proportion* ('Four Books on Human Proportion') Dürer makes an exhaustive study of human form and relative proportions, and his sketchbooks show that he had a continuing interest in the application of geometrical simplification as a method in preparatory drawing.

These techniques were adopted by several of his followers, notably Erhard Schön, who was a pupil and is known to have lived in Dürer's house for some years. Schön (1491–1542) became a prolific woodblock designer, producing a steady stream of religious and satirical prints for the mass market (often intentionally provocative).

Schön also went on to present his own ideas on art-theory in a volume entitled *Underweissung der Proportion* (Nuremberg, 1538). His and Dürer's device of reducing complex figures into more manageable geometric forms, particularly useful to

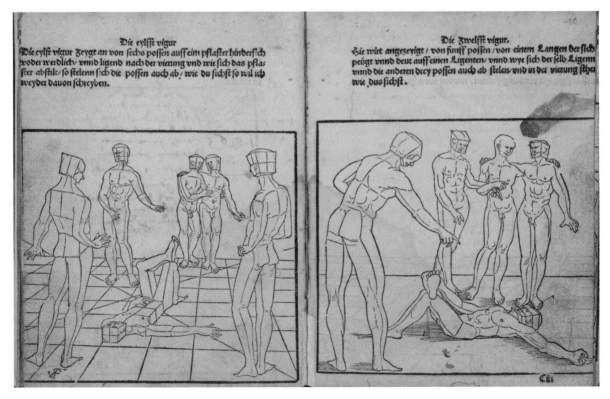

indicate perspective, became a standard drawing technique, but Schön's proto-cubist images have a strange, somewhat surreal, appeal of their own. The Italian artist Luca Cambiasi was another artist who used this technique of geometric simplification as a preparatory method to create his compositions.

Known as 'massing', this procedure was widely adopted, and is in fact still taught as a drawing technique, a transitional blocking-in to create visual weight in a composition.

*

'The total length and general axis of a standing body is determined by a basic vertical which runs from the heel of the standing leg to the top of the head, and goes through the pit of the stomach. The pelvis is inscribed in a trapezoid, and the thorax in a square (in some female figures in a vertical rectangle), and the axes of these, meeting at the pit of the stomach, are slightly shifted against the basic vertical. The knee of the standing leg, and thereby the length of both thighs, is found by bisecting the line which connects the hip-point with the lower terminal of the basic vertical. The head, if turned in full profile, is inscribed in a square, and the contours of the shoulders, hips and loins are determined by circular arcs.

(Quoted from Erwin Panovsky's classic biography *The Life and Art of Albrecht Dürer*, 1943).

LEFT: Pages from a book showing the geomtrizing of the human figure by Erhard Schön in *Underweissung der Proportion*, 1538.

RIGHT: *Five figures in a building*, woodcut by Erhard Schön in *Underweissung der Proportion*, 1538.

NUREMBERG: EARLY-MODERN CENTRE OF ENTERPRISE & CULTURE

Natural resource and location are the ultimate determinants of any town or region. Nuremberg, in the late medieval period was not particularly well endowed with the former, but it was located at the crossroads of several trade routes. These realities marked its character from the beginning; it owed its existence, and later prosperity, to its enterprise. The later medieval period saw the emergence of a whole range of new trades and industries in what was now an Imperial Free city. By the end of the Middle Ages, at the dawn of the Modern era, it was the foremost producer in the whole of Europe of finished metal products, including wire, household utensils, weapons and armour. In essence, it was at the forefront of an early phase of the Industrial Revolution. The demand for its products led to a sense of economic confidence, and Nuremberg became a vibrant and innovative manufacturing centre with strong links to other important European cities—particularly with Venice, which was an important trading partner.

It was inevitable, with its growing capacity to adopt novel technologies, that Nuremberg would become involved with the recently invented process of printing. In 1470, Anton Koberger, a Nuremberg patrician, started a printing-house that rapidly became the most successful in Germany. Others followed, and Nuremberg soon became a leading centre of printing and book production. It was also renowned for other 'high-tech' and luxury commodities, including scientific instruments—which were the reason that Regiomantanus (q.v.), and other important figures, chose to pursue their scientific investigations there. Albrecht Dürer was the most famous son of the town, and spent much of his creative life in Nuremberg, but many other important figures are associated with it. Martin Behaim, the creator of the first terrestrial globe, (1492) was born and worked in the town, as was Peter Helein, who manufactured the world's first pocket watch (1504). It is indicative of the spirit of the time and place that the text that shattered the medieval world-view, Nicolas Copernicus's iconoclastic *De Revolutionibus Orbium Celestium*, in which he proposed a heliocentric model of the universe, should be published in here in 1543.

Nuremberg was a principle centre of German Humanism, the intellectual movement associated with the revival of Classical knowledge, and on the religious front it played a prominent part in the Protestant Reformation (which was accepted by the town in 1525). In the Arts the city also had an important role, as the focus of the movement known as German Mannerism.

· NIL MELIUS ARTE ·

Nürnbergk

Neudorffer   *Jamitzer*

Arte nihil melius, nihil orbe salubrius arte; | *Est ea fida comes, comis amica, bonis.*

Nichts beſſers iſt, dann kunſt auff Erdn, | *Als Kunſt: Kunſt iſt ein trewer Gfehrt___,*
Nichts nützlichers kan gfunden werdn, | *Drumb ſeind Kunſtler allr Ehren wehrt.*

ABOVE: This engraving shows Wenzel Jamnitzer and the mathematician Johann Neudorffer at a table, with the city of Nuremberg in the background. Both are prominent citizens, and each in his different way is involved with geometrical figures. With Neudorffer, as a classical scholar, the emphasis is on the academic aspects of this study, whereas Jamnitzer, the practical master-craftsmen, is using his invention of a Perspectograph to delve into the artistic possibilities of geometry.

NUREMBERG, PLAGUE & WAR

Unfortunately, Nuremberg's vitality and its multiple concerns, as a trade hub, a centre of innovation and a focus of religious, philosophical and artistic ideas, led ultimately to its demise. Its geographic centrality, with traders and visitors constantly passing through the city, meant that it was particularly susceptible to less welcome visitations.

There were outbreaks of the Plague every few years between the middle and late 16th century that led to the deaths of thousands of its citizens; two of the artists featured here, Jamnitzer and Lencker, were victims of this disease in the 1585 outbreak. The Plague was persistent throughout Germany in the 16th century, and Nuremberg suffered outbreaks in 1405, 1435, 1437, 1482, 1494, 1520, 1534, 1552, 1556, 1562 and 1563 (nearby Augsburg was even more seriously affected, with more than 20 outbreaks during the 16th century).

These devastating events were later compounded by the social ravages of intensive religious strife. Nuremberg was thoroughly involved in the 30-years war (1618-1648) which had a particularly devastating effect on the town, after which it went into a something of a decline, from which it only really recovered in the 19th century.

PRINTING & PUBLISHING
IN THE RENAISSANCE

From its invention in Germany around the mid 15th century, the printing press, and the whole business of printed publication expanded at an extraordinary rate. Estimates vary, but nevertheless the statistics are quite remarkable. Within just fifty years, by 1500, there were as many as 1,000 print-shops in capitals throughout Europe, and these had produced something in the region of 40,000 editions, and up to 20 million books! The capacity of this new technology to create hundreds, even thousands, of identical texts had provided an unprecedented stimulus to intellectual life, one that had greatly facilitated study and debate. Texts were no longer an exclusive medium to be used by scholars for other scholars, but were available to all who could read and had the wherewithal to purchase the printed word. Books, pamphlets and prints soon became familiar, and in some cases, eminently collectable, items. Printing became an entirely new kind of occupation, the print-shop a new centre of intellectual exchange.

The range of topics covered in these early years of

ABOVE: Books, and their illustrations, were soon covering every imaginable topic.

printing is equally surprising. The first publications dealt mainly with religious subjects; Gutenberg's Bible was, of course, a very early production of the genre. But very soon, books on every imaginable subject were available. There were maps and travel books, scientific texts and medical manuals, treatises on warfare and fortification, on nature and cookery. Almanacs and sheet music soon appeared, as did pornography. Books proved to be very popular, particularly among the new monied mercantile classes—and they could be profitable to the entrepreneurs who were involved in their production. Cities like Nuremberg, Venice and Antwerp became notable centres of production. There was a negative side to the use of the new medium however. Both sides of the Catholic–Protestant schism used printed material to promote their cause, occasionally resulting in sensationalistic and violent propaganda. But in general the right to publish freely, without having to submit to state or church authorities, exerted a liberating influence and led to an unprecedented diffusion of ideas.

Printing presses were typically financed by private patrons, often with an eye for profit. But anyone with the means, or the cause, could set up their own press. Regiomontanus established a printing house in Nuremberg in 1471 to publish his own scientific ideas and those of others, making him the first scientific publisher; this was a noble precedent. Tycho Brahe printed his own works, as did Johannes Kepler, and Galileo's conflict with the Church was precipitated by the publication of his highly controversial scientific discoveries. Kepler commented that 'the number of authors whose writings are printed is now greater than the number of all the authors over the past thousand years'. Moreover, because these Renaissance authors had the nerve to challenge and contradict long-held beliefs printing became a powerful liberating and democratising influence. Other important innovations vie with printing as being responsible for the introduction of the modern era, including gunpowder and advances in navigational instruments, but the printing revolution, and the mass media that resulted, helped change human consciousness itself.

Gutenberg's Bible was not the first printed book, but his technical achievements established the

COPERNICUS'S *REVOLUTIONIBUS*

In 1543 the Nuremberg printer Johannes Petreius was offered, and went on to print, an obscure, highly technical astronomical treatise by the assistant of an equally obscure Polish scholar. The book proved to be one of the most radical and influential texts of its time, or since. Nicolas Copernicus's *De Revolutionibus Orbium Coelestium* ('On the Revolutions of the Celestial Spheres') was notoriously slow to gain acceptance, but this 200-page book, with an initial print-run of a mere 400 copies, managed to bring about one of the most profound changes in human thought in all of human history. Copernicus had written a draft of the *Revolutionibus* many years earlier, laying out his proposed revision to the long established, Earth-centred,

ABOVE: Nicolas Copernicus, the timid, but epoch-making astronomer.

Ptolemaic planetary system – but he was well aware of the furore that his theory might cause, so this initial thesis was circulated only among a few close academic friends. In his later years an ailing Copernicus was urged to publish by a young mathematician, Georg Joachim Rhetiticus, and he finally agreed shortly before he died. It is uncertain whether Copernicus ever actually saw a printed copy of his proposed alternative model of the Universe, but his concern about the reaction that it might provoke proved to be well-founded. His book challenged established religious authority, the accepted philosophical tradition and even ordinary experience – but it was scientifically sound, and the new medium of printing ensured that it was widely distributed and read, despite opposition from entrenched views. It created a slow-burning revolution, and the place of Man in the scheme of things was changed forever.

entire process and, importantly, set a high aesthetic standard for the printed word. The production of other Classic works soon followed; from an educational point of view, Euclid's *Elements* was among the most important. The *Elements* were first printed in Latin, in Venice, in 1482 (see opposite page). In the following century it was translated and published in a range of vernacular European languages - it was brought into Italian in 1543, German in 1558, French in 1565 and English in 1570. This mathematical masterpiece, which was written in Alexandria in North Africa around 300BC, having suffered from near-extinction in the West, was soon enjoying a circulation that would have been entirely unimaginable in the Ancient World.

ABOVE: The availability of high quality paper, around 1400, opened the possibilities of the printing revolution, which began with the use of a press adapted from the familiar wine-press, woodcut printing blocks and water-based inks. In the 1450s the entrepreneurial Johannes Gutenberg took the next great steps with his novel methods of re-useable type and oil-based inks. These innovations caught on very fast however, spreading from Mainz to Nuremberg by the 1460s, and to Italy around the same time.

Calendars and almanacs were some of the most popular and useful forms of early printed material. Ratdolt's *Kalendario*, which provided accurate information on the phases of the moon and the positions of the planets, based on Regiomontanus' calculations, was far superior to previous productions.

RATDOLT'S *EUCLID*

The publication of Euclid's *Elements*, in Venice, in 1482, is an important benchmark in the advance of mathematical knowledge, and in the history of the production of printed books. The *Elementorium Geometricum*, to give its full Latin title, was the master-work of a master-printer, Erhard Ratdolt. Ratdolt, the son of an Augsburg sculptor, moved to Venice for the opportunities that it provided in the burgeoning new field of quality printing.

The printing trade in Venice at this time, during the latter part of the 15th century, was dominated by Germans – there were around thirty of them in the city – but Ratdolt's productions were to prove exceptional, not least for their typographic decoration, which he virtually invented. He produced a *Kalendario* for Regiomontanus in 1482, which featured the first title-page of any book, and his *Elementorium* was the first printed book to be illustrated with mathematical figures, some six hundred in all, for which he devised a novel method of plate-making (using wire and plaster). Ratdolt also designed type, and managed to print using gold-leaf; he was a highly talented and original craftsman.

RIGHT: A page from Erhard Ratdolt's printed version of Euclid's *Elements*, for which he devised various innovations, including a new method of printing diagrams.

The *Elementorium* had been adapted from a medieval translation, by either Campanus (*q.v.*) or Adelard of Bath, both of whom had travelled to the Islamic world to acquire Arabic versions and made translations. Ratdolt's beautiful publication, just 27 years after Gutenberg had built his first printing press, was an immediate success, and was to prove enormously influential. Most importantly, it introduced the very notion of theoretical geometry to the receptive cultural milieu of the early Renaissance. Dürer, who visited and stayed in Venice, was among many who were deeply impressed by this beautifully produced book. It took until 1543, for an Italian translation to appear in print, and 1558 for a German edition. Not surprisingly Ratdolt's version of Euclid became the model of subsequent mathematical book design.

LEFT: Pages from *Shpaera Mundi*.

SPHAERA MUNDI

Ratdolt was interested in astronomy as well as mathematical science and clearly had a mission to use the new method of printing to communicate knowledge on these subjects. As well as producing a *Kalendario* for Regiomontanus he published this treatise on the sphere by the 13th century English astronomer Sacrobosco (John Holybush). As with his other printed books, the *Sphaera Mundi* is beautifully illustrated with a decorative title-page and woodcut ornamental initials; this was also the first book to have been printed with three-colour pages.

Sacrobosco is a rather obscure Medieval scholar; the *Sphaera*, 1230, is essentially a dissertation on the Ptolemaic planetary system (probably based on Gerard of Cremona's translation from the Arabic), and he is also notable for having written a popular introduction to the Hindu-Arabic number system. Both of these works were recommended reading for the next four centuries.

GEOMETRICAL TREATISES
IN GERMANY IN THE 1500s

The success of Dürer's 'Instruction manuals for artists' (which soon ran to several editions) led others to follow his example and produce similar works of their own. Dürer's two books set the tone and subject matter for this new genre, and although many are interesting on their own account, none that followed were quite as ambitious or comprehensive, in a purely didactic sense, as the original. Dürer's books included sections on plane geometry, polyhedra, on proportional canons of the human body, on architectonic forms, on typography, and of course on the principles of perspective. His successors tended to select just one or two of these themes – and there are marked differences in the ways they handle them. Although they all present themselves as teaching manuals, and many include basic primers on geometry, there are a variety of different approaches – and some of the more interesting seem intent on using the form to demonstration their own skills and imagination.

As indicated in the Introduction to this book, little is known about these post-Dürer artist/authors. Many of them, like the master himself, seem to have been native to Nuremberg, or at least came to live there, and most had a background in one or other of the crafts. Jamnitzer, Lautensack and Lencker

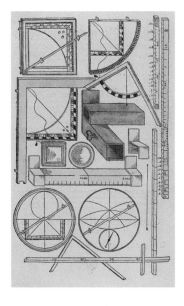

LEFT: *Measuring tools* from Walther Hermann Ryff's *Architetura*, 1543

were goldsmiths (as was Dürer's own father); Hirschvogel was originally a glass painter, Stoer a master-carpenter. Their books all tend to focus on the geometrical aspects of art, in which they try to combine older, craft usage of geometry with a more academic and theoretical kind, including theories on perspective – and they all wrote in the German vernacular.

The background to these all of these productions was the popularity and commercial success of books and prints in general at this time. Competitive pressures within this thriving market had led to improving standards of production, with illustrations in particular achieving very high levels of accuracy and clarity. In fact the printing revolution was making a profound impact on art itself, with many artists achieving international recognition through the medium of engraved and woodcut prints. Dürer was in the forefront of this elevation of print into an art form. In his forties, he decided to concentrate on printmaking and created the brilliant series that ensured his, and the forms, reputation — and made him fairly wealthy in the process. Dürer's preoccupation with the role of geometry as it might provide a scientific and theoretical foundation to the *artes liberal* was equally influential.

Largely as a result of this influence a certain fashion for geometry developed in early 16th Germany; a style that accorded with the new rationalising mood of the Renaissance. In fact the concept of properly measuring and accurately representing the physical world had taken hold in many quarters; this was a period that saw great advances in such diverse areas as astronomy, surveying, cartography, optical lens making and the manufacture of scientific instruments of all kinds. There were many connections between science, art and the crafts in this broad movement, and to engage with it, if only by purchasing one of the many available treatises on geometry and perspective, was to be associated with the new spirit of enquiry that seemed intent on uncovering the hidden structure of the world; the new magic of Science.

JOST AMMAN: MASTER ENGRAVER

The engravings for Jamnitzer's *Perspectiva Corporum Regularium* were cut by Jost Amman, an incredibly talented and prolific woodblock-cutter, with a long association with the author. Amman came to Nuremberg from Zurich in 1560, where he first worked as an apprentice in the workshop of the renowned print-maker Virgil Solis, and then with Wentzel Jamnitzer; his initials actually appear on eleven of the engravings in the *Perspectiva*. He went on to become a well-known illustrator in his own right, with more than fifty books to his credit. Amazingly, at the same time that Amman was engraving Jamnitzer's opus he was working on another volume, *Das Standebuch* ('The Book of Trades', Nuremberg, 1568), an extensive survey of contemporary crafts and occupations that featured no fewer than 106 engravings (see opposite). This appeared in the same year as the *Perspectiva*. Jost Amman's extraordinary productivity is indicated by a reported remark made by of one of his pupils that his work over a particular four-year period would have filled a hay wagon. Amman stayed in Nuremberg till the end of his life in 1591; his studio is believed to have produced upwards of 1500 prints.

LEFT AND BELOW: From Jost Amman's *Das Standebuch* ('Book of Trades'), published in 1568. Among its 114 woodcuts, which have accompanying verses by Hans Sachs, are these images that depict various aspects of the printing trade.

RIGHT: Detail showing a woodblock cutter ('*formschneider*') at work; woodcut by Jost Amman.

THE POPULARISERS: RODLER, HIRSCHVOGEL & LAUTENSACK

Among the earlier authors to emulate Dürer was his one-time student Hieronymus Rodler. Just three years after Dürer's death, in 1531, Rodler produced a booklet with the declared aim of making Dürer's ideas more comprehensible. This short work focuses on the use of perspective in drawing; woodcuts show simple drawings of interiors and exteriors of a working craft environment to

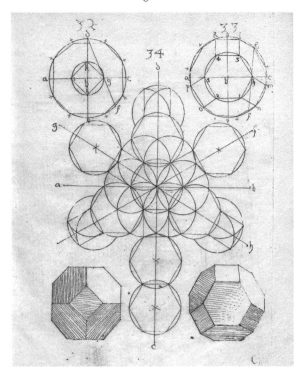

ABOVE: Diagram from Augustin Hirschvogel's 'Ein aigentliche und grundliche anweysung in die Geometria', Nuremberg, 1543.

illustrate his theory but, uncharacteristically, there is no mention of plane or solid geometry, and no examples of regular figures at all. Far from Dürer's sophisticated approach, Rodler's work conveys an almost naïve simplicity.

By contrast, Augustine Hirschvogel (1503–1553), produced a very serious treatise entitled *Ein aigentliche und grundliche anweysung in die Geometria* ('An original and thorough instruction in Geometry', Nuremberg, 1543) which was primarily concerned with polyhedra. His book actually improved on Dürer's in this respect by showing the constructions of an extended range of solid figures, together with alternate perspective views – he investigates the semi-regular Archimedean as well as the regular Platonic solids. This was a thoroughly workmanlike manual, and is clearly intended to be a practical aid to all those engaged in the crafts or architectural trades.

Hirschvogel was born in Nuremberg, into a family of glass painters, and his career, in which he became a mathematician and cartographer as well as a famous printmaker, epitomises the possibilities for artistic and social mobility of his time. When Nuremberg adopted the Protestant Reformation the demand for stained glass came to an end and the Hirschvogel workshop, of necessity, had to seek commissions in other areas. The talented Augustin first applied his talents to cartography, at which he excelled. He was soon producing maps of Austria for the Imperial Court of Vienna and also became known for his 'Views of Vienna', which included a city plan, in which he employed perspective, and the novel method of triangulation, which he devised himself. In his use of mathematics, accurate surveying and perspective for these representations of the city Hirschvogel is part of a tradition that traces directly back to Dürer, who recommends the use of scientific instruments for just this purpose in his *Underweysung*.

Heinrich Lautensack, who produced an 'Instruction on the use of compass and straightedge in perspective and proportion', (*Des Circles und Richtscheyts*, Augsburg, 1564) continued this move towards more accurate standards of representation. His manual adopts the agenda set by Dürer. It gives a primer on linear geometry and methods for the construction of regular and semi-regular solids, deals with the theory of perspective, and proposes systems of proportion for the human body and horses. Like Rodler's and Hirschvogel's books of the two previous decades it is a worthy, serious production, if a little dull, and was clearly intended as a guide for artists and craftsmen and nothing more. But a series of volumes were about to appear that were to use the Geometrical/Perspective treatise format in more imaginative ways.

ABOVE: Perspective drawings from Hieronymus Rodler's '*Ein schön nutzlich Buchlein*', 1531.

ABOVE: Guide to the proportionate drawing of the human body: from Heinrich Lautensack's '*Des Circles und Richtscheyts*', Nuremberg, 1564.

IV

POLYHEDRA
and the
CREATIVE
IMAGINATION

Mid-sixteenth Germany saw the
publication of a handful of books that
presented a range of
geometrically-inspired illustrations
essentially unlike anything that had
appeared before, or have been seen since.
This is Geometry-in-Art
at its most intense.

LEFT: A pen and watercolour drawing of a fantastical architectural setting with polyhedra and figures, two of whom are carrying measuring instruments. This is the largest surviving example of Lorenz Stoer's work. Although it appears to be a title-page it's actual intended use is uncertain. Since it is multi-chrome in the original it was clearly not intended for publication in this form - possibly it was an attempt to persuade a patron to fund some larger scheme.

THE GERMAN CREATIVE GEOMETRICISTS

With this group of author/artists we arrive at an extraordinary, if short-lived, phase of geometric creativeness. It seems very likely that each of this group knew, or at the very least, was familiar with each other's work – and they would certainly have known the more prosaic Geometric/Perspective treatises of the recent past. But their productions are of a different order of artistic imagination. There was nothing as original as their inventive drawings in any previous manuals, and although these authors exerted a certain influence, there was nothing quite as interesting in anything that followed. This brief flowering of creativity came from an art-fellowship that seems scarcely to have been aware of its own existence as such. Although the ostensible purpose of their books was didactic, namely, to demonstrate methods of geometry and perspective, there is little attempt in any of them to convey an actual theory of perspective, relying instead on the 'evidence' of their own drawings – which are themselves far more imaginative than in any previous treatises. It is hard to avoid the conclusion that this group are, artistically speaking, playing with this genre. They seem to be tapping in to the wider appeal for this form that had been generated by their predecessors. And the books they produced were certainly popular; they were translated, reprinted and, in Jamnitzer's case, repeatedly pirated.

For a variety of reasons there will always be uncertainties about this brief flowering of geometric art and the group of artists that produced it. In the first place, as we have seen, the lives of the artists are themselves obscure; in addition none of them, apparently, had a great deal to say about their work; and to compound these deficits, a great deal of information and material evidence may have been lost in the turmoil of war and pestilence that descended on their homeland during and shortly after their time.

We do know that, sadly, both Jamnitzer and Lencker were victims of the plague that hit Nuremberg in 1585. The city had, in fact, seen repeated outbreaks of this dread disease since the first massive epidemic in 1437–50. In fact, war, religious turmoil and sporadic recurrences of the plague were part of the background of Germany at that time. It is difficult these days for us to imagine the devastation and disruption of ordinary life that these unwelcome events must have created – one of the side-effects must have been periodic suspensions of trade and travel. For our artist-craftsmen such interruptions may have presented a serious threat to their livelihood, but it could also have left them with time on their hands. Could this have been a factor in the creation of

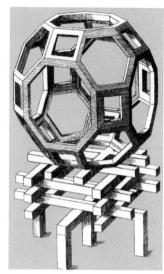

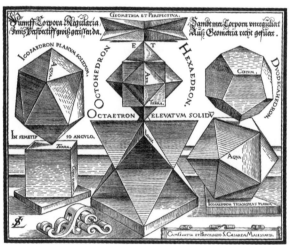

ABOVE LEFT: From Wenzel Jamnitzer's *Perspectiva Corporum Regularium*, 1568.

ABOVE RIGHT: From Peter Halt's *Perspectivische Reiss Kunst*, 1625.

LEFT: From an alternative title-page to Lorenz Stoer's *Geometria et Perspectiva*, c. 1567.

at least some of these drawings? There are many precedents of artistic creativity under conditions of enforced isolation and temporary exile. Boccaccio's *Decameron* was written while he and a group of friends were seeking refuge from the plague in a villa outside Florence. And Dürer's first trip to Italy was prompted by a similar motive, to escape the plague that had struck Nuremberg in 1498.

All the artist/authors who followed in Dürer's footsteps, as these certainly did, were caught up as he was with the consuming interest of the time,

namely, the methodological problems of realistic representation. Their books and drawings were in part a demonstration of this rationalising approach, and many of them used technical devices to assist them in their drawings – and it is certainly the case that they were successful in their representation of complex subjects. For these artists the clarity of representation that they desired (and frequently achieved) was completely in accord with the Platonic purity of their subject matter.

THE GERMAN CREATIVE GEOMETRICISTS 143

WENZEL JAMNITZER

Wenzel Jamnitzer (1508–1585) might lay claim to be the founding-figure of this group of mid-16th century German Geometricists. His work is the most assured and schematised, and he was the best known in his own time, but even here biographical details are rather limited. He originally came to Nuremberg from Vienna, and acquired citizenship in 1534. By the time he turned his attention to *Perspectiva Corporum Regularium* in 1568, he had chalked up a long, successful career as a goldsmith. He was, in fact, the leading goldsmith of his day, and the family workshop that he headed had made precious objects for many European royal courts, including four Habsburg Emperors. He became known as the 'German Cellini', and attained the position of Master of the Mint in Nuremberg, making him a very notable figure indeed in the town. Jamnitzer was also known to have been interested in scientific problems, to have made scientific instruments and published work on these matters. But the *Perspectiva* is in a different category; although it reflects both his craft skills and his scientific interests, it is essentially a work of pure geometric fantasy.

It is intriguing to speculate on Jamnitzer's conscious intentions in this book. It is clear that he was fully aware of Platonic notions of the 'elemental' symbolism associated with the regular solids, and he explicitly based his figures on the 13th book of Euclid and on Plato's *Timaeus* – but he seems to have had his own cosmological ideas of their correspondence with the physical world. As far as can be determined (since he never managed to complete his Introduction), he intended the scheme in the *Perspectiva* to present some sort of 'metaphorical alphabet' in which the five regular solids corresponded to the 5 Greek vowels, and the 24 variations of the solids corresponded to the 24 letters of that alphabet. This 'method never before employed', as he described it, would result in the 'avoidance of all superfluity and, in contrast to the old-fashioned way of teaching, no line or point will be drawn needlessly'. There is a clear resonance here to Plato's notion of the five regular solids as the basis of the phenomenal world, but it is a thoroughly idiosyncratic interpretation, in which he seems to have envisioned the generation of endless solid figures of various shapes and sizes as a metaphor for the creation of the physical world.

The second part is rather less schematic, or perhaps the scheme is less obvious. It begins with ten pairs of transparent, or skeletised, regular solids 'in the Italian manner', followed by six pages of spherical variations; then there are four pairs of

ABOVE: A portrait of Wentzel Jamnitzer by the Flemish painter Nicolas Neufchatel. Jamnitzer is holding proportional dividers in his right hand and an assaying device of his own making in the other.

pyramidal/conical variants, and the collection is finished off with three plates of rotundas, based on the *mazzocchio*, that staple of perspective treatises. Quite how these drawings are meant to fit into his scheme is not explained, but one suspects that they are simply effusions of Jamnitzer's extraordinary imagination. The engravings for *Perspectiva Corporum Regularium* were cut by Jost Amman (*q.v.*), an incredibly talented and prolific engraver, with a long association with Jamnitzer.

In his time Wenzel Jamnitzer was the most famous goldsmith in Europe, and many of the productions of his workshop can still be seen in museums across Europe. But these ornate *objets*, somewhat over-decorated with semi-precious stones, corals and shells, project an entirely different aesthetic impression from the geometric purity of the *Perspectiva Corporum*, which has been described as a 'visual fugue composed to the glory of the harmony of the Universe'.

ABOVE: Wentzel Jamnitzer with his Perspectival Machine, an engraving by Jost Amman. There is little indication here of Jamnitzer as an important figure in Nuremberg society with an international reputation as a Master Goldsmith. He is rather presented as an artist-scientist, operating the perspective device that he presumably used in creating his remarkably accurate drawings. In part this was probably a conscious redefinition of identity, away from that of a mere artisan towards the role of a Renaissance scholar.

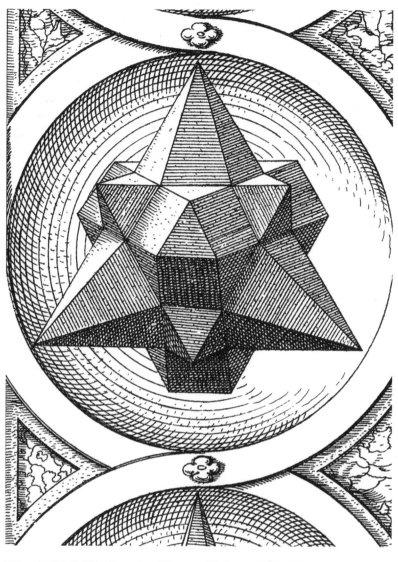

LEFT & BELOW: The underlying principle in Jamnitzer's drawings is derived from the Platonic notion of these solids as 'elements', i.e. Earth, Air, Fire and Water, and thereby as the foundation of physical reality. Jamnitzer himself felt that he had succeeded both in 'inventing a method of perspective' and 'the study of elementary forces'.

The scheme that he has adopted, at least for the polyhedral variations in first part of his book, is somewhat idiosyncratic. In the first place, each solid was ascribed a vowel (A for the tetrahedron, E for the octahedron, I for the cube, O for the icosahedron, U for the dodecahedron). Every solid/vowel section has 24 illustrations; the solid itself followed by 23 variations — and the number of variations are thought to have been determined by the 24 letters of the Greek alphabet Jamniter uses facets, truncations and stellations to produce 120 variations, twenty-four of each solid.

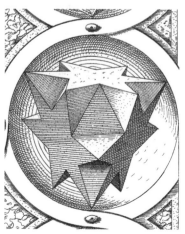

RIGHT: Details from tetrahedral, cubic and octahedral variants in Wenzel Jamnitzer's *Perspectiva Corporum Regularium*, Nuremberg, 1568.

ABOVE: Star icosahedral variants from pages F4 (left) and F5 (right) in Wenzel Jamnitzer's *Perspectiva Corporum Regularium*.

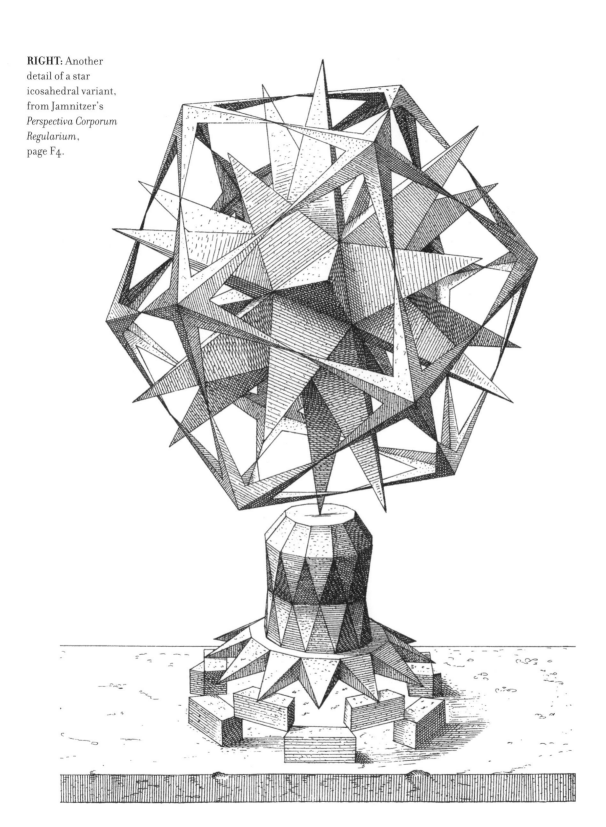

RIGHT: Another detail of a star icosahedral variant, from Jamnitzer's *Perspectiva Corporum Regularium*, page F4.

Conical variants from Jamnitzer's
Perspectiva Corporum Regularium .

RIGHT: plate no.H2

BELOW: plate no.H4

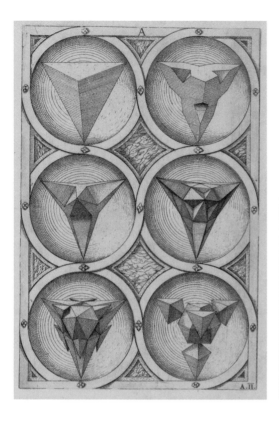

Plates from Wenzel Jamnitzer's *Perspectiva Corporum Regularium.*

ABOVE LEFT: A2 Tetrahedral variants.

ABOVE RIGHT: C1 Cubic variants.

BELOW: D4 and D5 Dodecahedral variants.

LORENZ STOER

Lorenz Stoer was the second of three Nuremberg artist to have published a geometric/perspective book around the years 1567–8. However, Stoer's *Geometria et Perspectiva* cannot be considered as a teaching aid by any stretch of the imagination since it is quite short, consisting of just eleven drawings, and has no text at all. It is, though, a most intriguing work. It features a series of geometric solids, some regular, balanced one on top of the other, set among various landscapes of overgrown, half-ruined buildings. Sometimes these geometrical and architectonic forms are accompanied by strange, trellised scrollwork. On his title page Stoer suggests that these drawings might be useful as patterns for *intarsia* (marquetry panels), although no examples have survived to indicate that these particular drawings were ever used for this purpose. Devoid of human or animal figures, they convey a rather melancholy, almost post-apocalyptic atmosphere – the 'eternal' qualities of the solid figures are emphasised by the ruined, abandoned

appearance of the cityscapes. Could this in part be a reflection of the devastating effects of the plague, and the fears of further visitations? Nuremberg and Augsburg had both suffered from a series of outbreaks of this dread disease throughout the 16th century, the most recent in 1563, just 3–4 years before this book was published. The drawings certainly have a haunted feeling about them, but the Renaissance had seen a revival of interest in classical ruins, they had began to be surveyed and measured, and were included in other perspective treatises, so Stoer's use of this subject-matter is far from unique.

Stoer also produced two remarkable folios of a whole series of geometric figures. Because they were in colour it is unlikely that these ever were intended to be published; one contains thirty-three paintings, the other three hundred and thirty-six. These delicate watercolours are clearly a labour of love. Several of the drawings in the latter collection have dates, indicating that they were produced over

OPPOSITE PAGE: This is the title page to Lorenz Stoer's 'Geometria er Perspectiva', Nuremberg, 1567. The subtitle indicates that these 'diverse designs of ruined buildings' might be useful to intarsia workers, and to amateurs. In the original the oval band contains the ambiguous epigram 'Who would do right by everyone? No one would even try'.

ABOVE: Plate no.1 from Stoer's *Geometria et Perspectiva*.

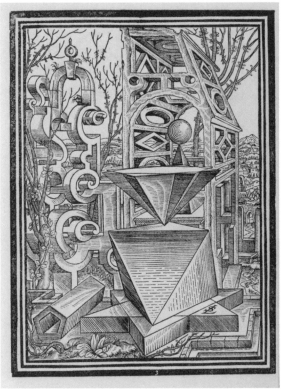

OPPOSITE AND ABOVE: Plates no. 2-8 from Stoer's *Geometria et Perspectiva*.

The Renaissance tradition of interest in ruins went back to Brunelleschi and Donatello, for whom it was associated with the Classical revival. This linkage continued with the architect Sebastiano Serlio, who included views of ruins in his work on perspective. But there was also a tradition of idealised ruins, particularly among printmakers from the Low countries.

a near forty-year period, from 1562 to the end of the century. Bound together around 1600, they present an extraordinarily beautiful collection of inventive geometric forms, and are the remarkable evidence of a sustained enthusiasm of a refined geometricism.

Until relatively recently Lorenz Stoer was mainly known for the 11 woodcuts shown here.

More recently, other drawings have come to light, including a folio of 336 delicate watercolours in the University Library in Munich that, according to the dates on some of them, seem to have been put together over a period of thirty-plus years. Very little is known of this artist/craftsman's life other than that he was born and spent much of his early life in Nuremberg. No text accompanies the woodcut prints in the slender volume in which they appear, and no explanation has survived that might throw light on his general fascination with regular geometric figures.

Stoer's woodcuts in *Geometria et Perspectiva* consist of various fanciful combinations of regular and figures and scrollwork (*rollwerk*), set in a somewhat haunted, ruined landscape. In the subtitle

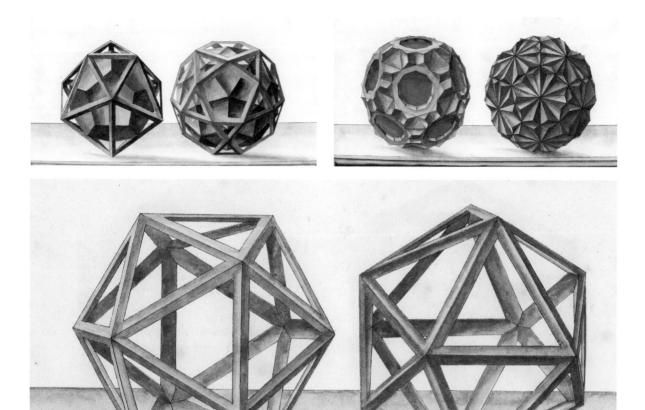

ABOVE: Three pages from Lorenz Stoer's watercolour series
Geometria et Perspectiva: Corpora regulata et irregulata.

to this short book Stoer suggests that these drawings
may be useful to cabinet-makers for *intarsia*
decoration and to 'amateurs'. He later moved to
Augsburg, which was a centre that specialised in
this craft, which rather confirms this idea, but no
direct adaptations of his work in this medium have
survived, and his drawings are of rather higher
quality than existing examples of inlaid panels.
There is some evidence that printed drawings were
used for this purpose at the time, but it is uncertain
whether Stoer's designs were ever taken up.

Despite the titles of his book and folio
manuscript, there is no attempt in either to teach

perspective, in fact the perspective that he uses is
not particular convincing. It seems clear though that
Stoer's underlying motivation is the same as Dürer's
before him, namely to elevate the standing of the arts
and crafts (and the artist's and craftsmen's social
standing) through the adoption of mathematical and
philosophical concepts.

Whatever else was happening in his life, Stoer
continued with his depiction of geometric figures
over the next 40 years, through a very unsettled
period of German history. His persistence is both
a tribute to his own dedication and to the enduring
fascination of this genre.

ABOVE LEFT:
Watercolour
no.243 from
*Geometria et
Perspectiva:
Corpora regulata et
irregulata.*

ABOVE RIGHT:
Watercolour
no.331 from
*Geometria et
Perspectiva:
Corpora regulata et
irregulata.*

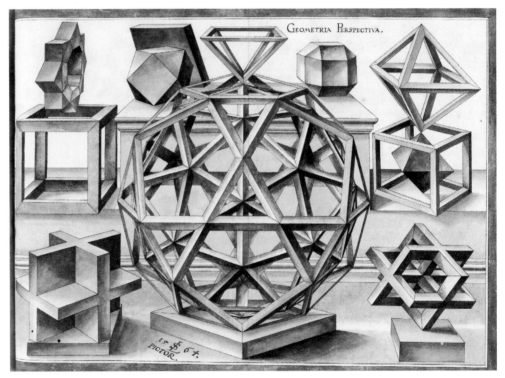

GEOMETRIA PERSPECTIVA.

ABOVE: Watercolour no.332 from
*Geometria et Perspectiva: Corpora regulata
et irregulata.*

OPPOSITE PAGE: from *Geometria et
Perspectiva: Corpora regulata et irregulata.*

GEOMETRICA ET PERSPECTIVA CORPORA REGVLATA ET IRREGVLATA,

ANON (*c.* 1565–1600)
GEOMETRISCHE UND PERSPECTIVISCHE

The following geometrical drawings are from another folio, by an anonymous hand, containing 36 watercolours in all, and are broadly similar in style to the other artists featured in this section. Using pen and watercolour, these, like Lorenz Stoer's, were apparently drawn over an extended period. Many are clearly derived from Jamnitzer and Lencker, others have an original eccentricity all of their own. An endearing, and distinctive, feature is the inclusion of small creatures of various kinds.

Jamnitzer's and Lencker's books had a broader appeal than previous perspective treatises, and established the genre – but Stoer's later work and that of this anonymous artist seem to have been more private productions; it is possible that they were commissioned, but more likely that they were simply drawn for personal satisfaction.

The series begins with drawings of Platonic solids, as a sort of declaration of intent, and goes on to explore similar themes to those of the previous artists, and clearly borrows from them. Indeed, the similarities between the range of subject matter of these drawings and those of the other artists featured in this book begs various questions that unfortunately can never be answered – how close were their relationships, and how familiar were they with each other's work? Under what circumstances were these illustrations produced? One would love to know more details of their day-to-day lives. What we can be sure of is that the calm, contemplative qualities of these images must have contrast strongly with what is known of the politically turbulent and pestilential backdrop of the times in which they were created. In Germany, in the later 16th century, an artist might be forgiven in seeking refuge from the troubled world through the contemplation of eternal Platonic forms.

OPPOSITE: Pages 45, 61, 49 & 53 from an album, *Geometrische und Perspectivische Zeichnungen*, by an anonymous artist.

ANON (*c*.1565–1600): *GEOMTRISCHE UND PERSPECTIVISCHE*

LEFT: Page 79
from the album
*Geometrische und
Perspectivische
Zeichnungen*, by an
anonymous artist.

JOHANNES LENCKER

Johannes Lencker (1523–1585), was a near-contemporary of Wenzel Jamnitzer and had much else in common with him. He too was a well-known goldsmith and a notable citizen of Nuremberg and, like Jamnitzer, played a prominent role in its civil life. He is also known to have been involved in devising measuring and drawing instruments, including those he employed in creating his treatise *Perspectiva Literaria*, 1567 (see following). Much of *Perspectiva Literaria* is taken up with perspective drawings of capital letters, 'as if cut from metal or wood', but it finishes with an imaginative series of drawings of architectonic and polyhedral forms, including an embellished *Nautilus* shell. Some of these are similar enough to Jamnitzer's drawings to indicate a close familiarity, although Lencker's 1567 book actually came out in the year before Jamnitzer's *Perspectiva Corporum Regularium*. Whatever the intentions of this work, and whatever was going on generally in the minds of those involved in the production of each of these collections of geometrically-based drawings, it is clear that there is a distinct sharing of style and visual ideas, even if they did not amount to a 'school'.

A few years later, in 1571, Lencker produced a new book, simply called *Perspectiva*, that provided more explicit instructions on the use of perspective than the earlier work. In this, Lencker makes a distinction between the 'high, beautiful and subtle art' of perspective as a philosophical theory and his own more practical approach to the subject. He makes it clear that he is concerned only with correct proportional representation. This volume also presents an interesting series of sketches depicting what one imagines was a fairly comprehensive survey of the instruments used in surveying and drawing at the time.

Lencker's books on perspective, together with his technical, instrument-making abilities, gave him an entrée to the *Kunstkammer* of the Electors of Saxony at Dresden (see pgs.172-173), and commissions from the courts at Kassel and Munich. A folio of his watercolour drawings, dated to 1576, is held at the *Kupferstich-Kabinett* in Dresden. These charming drawings are similar in subject-matter to Jamnitzer's geometric fantasies. His work in general is confident and intriguing, the pity is that this artist produced so little, or that so little has survived. Lencker, together with Jamnitzer, died of the Plague that struck Nuremberg in 1585.

ABOVE LEFT: The title-page of Lorenz Stoer's *Perspectiva*, 1571.

ABOVE RIGHT AND LEFT: Two pages from Johannes Lencker's *Perspectief Buch*, a folio made during his stay at the court of Saxony in Dresden, *c.*1576.

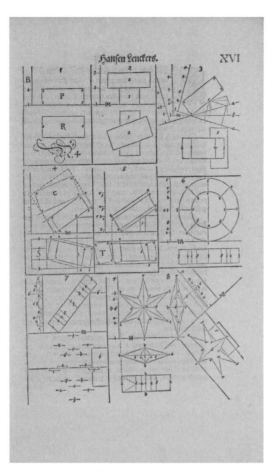

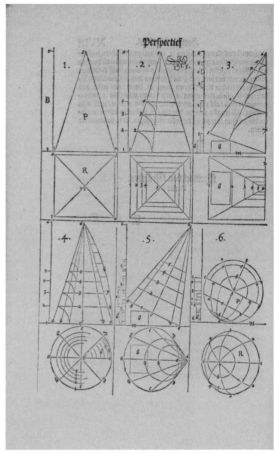

ABOVE LEFT AND RIGHT AND OPPOSITE PAGE ABOVE:
Perspectival images together with drawing and surveying
instruments from Johannes Lenckers's 'Perspectiva' of 1571. All
part of 'his complex understanding of perspective' according
to James Elkins.

RIGHT AND OPPOSITE PAGE RIGHT: Semi-regular figures
from Johannes Lencker's *Perspectiva*, 1571.

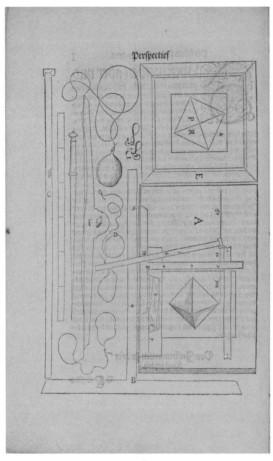

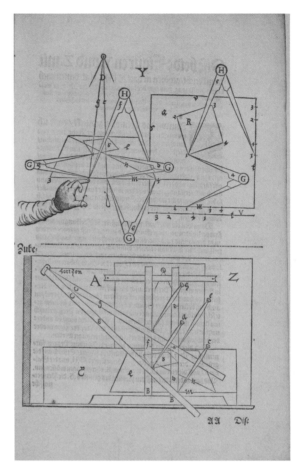

LETTERS & PERSPECTIVE:
PERSPECTIVA LITERARIA

Consisting, as it does, of the letters of the entire alphabet in various perspectival postures, Johannes Lencker's *'Perspectiva Literaria'* must rank as one of the more curious examples of the Geometric/Perspective genre (although it also has several interesting semi-regular forms). Lencker's use of letters in various attitudes, to

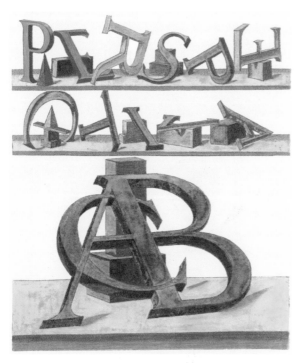

ABOVE: The first page from Johannes Lencker's *Perspectiva Literaria*, 'Perspective of Letters', Nuremberg, 1567.

demonstrate perspective and the application of his own 'perspective machine', was entirely original, although this theme was taken up again by Lucas Brunn, the curator of the Dresden *Kunstkammer*, in his own perspective treatise in 1613 (see below).

Lencker, like Jamnitzer, was trained as a goldsmith, and he too went on to become an important figure in the town politics of Nuremberg. Unfortunately, not much else is known of his life. His drawings of geometrical figures clearly owe something to Jamnitzer, and he is a better draughtsman than Stoer, his figures are more freely drawn than either of these. Unlike Jamnitzer, there is no attempt to fit these drawings into any schema, other than the alphabet itself. In fact he presents his illustrations as 'evidence in themselves' of perspective principles. It seems that, in common with Dürer, he had a good understanding of the basic principles of Optics and is known to have developed measuring and perspectival instruments, illustrated in a later work that is simply entitled *'Perspectiva'*.

The *'Literaria'*, however, with its three-dimensional drawings of letters, is not accompanied by any explanation of his intentions. There were, of course, precedents for the proper forming of the letters of the alphabet in art/craft treatises; both Pacioli and Dürer

ABOVE AND BELOW: Further illustrations from Johannes Lencker's *Perspectiva Literaria* ,'Perspective of Letters', Nuremberg, 1567. Lencker's technical skills, in both drawing and devising perspective instruments, took him to the Courts of Saxony in Dresden and later to Munich. For Lencker the *Perspectiva Literaria* was a conscious attempt to reveal the perspective constructions that had been 'hidden' in his earlier work, *Perspectiva* of 1571.

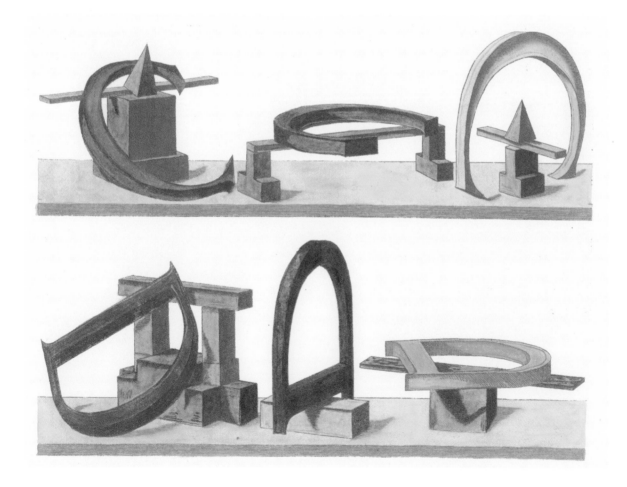

dealt with them in their books, and they subsequently became a stock theme in this literature. But Lencker brought perspective and lettering together, showing all the letters of the alphabet in a whole variety of positions. The book was meant to dazzle with its demonstration of drawing ability and knowledge of perspective; it was very popular when first published and manages to retain a certain appeal to the modern viewer.

*

Lucas Brunn is known as the curator of the Dresden *Kunstkammer*, having been appointed as the Court Mathematician sometime before 1620. He later produced a German language edition of Euclid's *Elements* (Nuremberg, 1625). His use of letters to demonstrate how perspective drawings may be produced without the use of models, using a 'perspective machine', is clearly linked to Lencker's work in this area. He must have known Lencker, who had spent some time himself as a tutor in the Dresden *Kunstkammer*, but the details of their association are, unfortunately, lost.

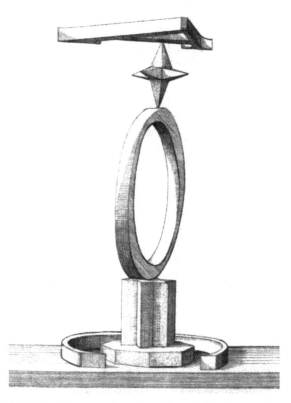

ABOVE: An illustration from Lucas Brunn's *Praxis Perspectivae* (which was clearly influenced by Hans Lencker's *Perpectiva Literaria*);. On the basis of this work Brunn, a Professor of mathematics and instrument-maker from Nuremberg, became the court mathematician and curator at the Electoral *Kunstskammer* in Dresden (see following pages).

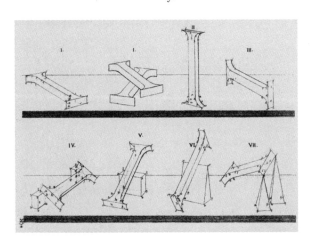

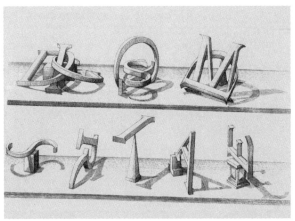

ABOVE LEFT AND RIGHT: Illustrations from Lucas Brunn's *Praxis Perspectivae* published in Nuremberg in 1615, in which he describes Optics as ' the noblest, highest and most sensible discipline.

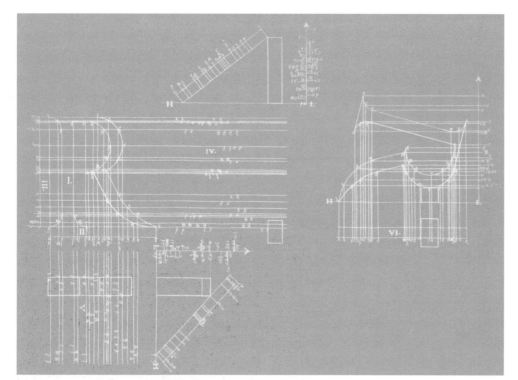

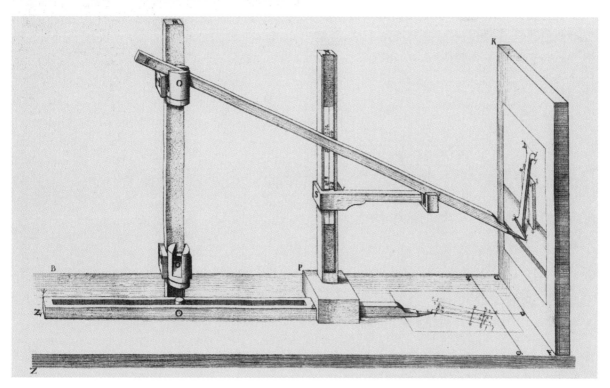

ABOVE: Lucas Brunn's 'perspective machine'.

THE DRESDEN *KUNSTSKAMMER*

In the 16th scientific instruments of all kinds were highly valued, and were often seen as objects worthy of collection. They were in fact occasionally presented as high-prestige gifts to the various Courts, and many such gifts were retained in the princely collections known as *Kunstkammers*, (Chambers of Arts). Some of these *Kunstkammers* were mere accumulations of curiosities while others were far more serious, dedicated collections. The most famous example of the latter was housed at the Dresden Court in Saxony, which was regarded as one of the finest of its kind in the whole of Europe. It held an extensive collection of objects of scientific interest, including tools and technical instruments, many of which had been commissioned. This was a sort of prototype Science Museum, and attracted some very illustrious visitors, including Johannes Kepler, who is known to have visited the institution around 1600. Kepler witnessed a demonstration of a *camera obscura* here, which made a great impression on him, and he saw a model of a dodecahedron, which is said to have inspired his meditation on the symmetry of snowflakes, the *Strena*.

The curator of this establishment, from 1619, was the court mathematician Lucas Brunn (1572–1628), an outstanding figure in his own right. Brunn had come to Dresden from Nuremberg where, as a

ABOVE: The fine turning of ivories was regarded as a worthy occupation for aristocrats since, by engaging in this activity, the princely student could engage with matter and in so doing acquire a better understanding of Nature.

professor of mathematics, he had published a treatise on Perspective, *Praxis Perspectivae* (1613) which was influenced by Hans Lencker's *Perpectiva Literaria*. He was also a maker of astronomical instruments and, since he was thoroughly familiar with the most recent developments in optics, was an obvious candidate for the post of curator to the *Kunstkammer*. The Elector of Saxony, Rudolph II, was personally interested in the subject, having conducted his own experiments with lenses and mirrors. In the finest tradition of the Renaissance polymaths, Brunn produced a German edition of Euclid in 1625, in the preface of which he declared that 'geometry and the study of proportion form a lofty and necessary art', and praised the Saxon Electors for their patronage of the *Kunstkammer*. An inventory of the library of this enlightened institution has shown that it held the works of Dürer, Jamnitzer, Lencker, Lautensack and Hirschvogel, and many other volumes on perspective and geometry.

*

Lencker's and Brunn's drawings may have appealed to the Electors of Saxony as supplying inspiration for their own work in creating geometrical *objets d'art* from precious and exotic materials. This tradition, of princely involvement in the use of lathes and other specialised tools in the creation of fine *objets*, was regarded as uplifting to a noble spirit. The engagement with materiality, even of such a refined kind, that was required by this activity was seen as a useful addition to a prince's education; 'The pursuit of this art reveals the wonderful work of nature to the eyes'. The courtly environment at the Dresden *Kunstkammer*, with its aristocratic interest in the more recent discoveries in science, was very encouraging for serious scholars – in particular for the study of mathematics and optics. Brunn's perspective device and drawings were included among its extensive collection of astronomical, optical and geometrical instruments.

ABOVE: The production of elaborate turnings became an accepted form of manual activity among the higher classes: page from *Recueil d'ouvrages curieux de mathematiques et de mechanique* by Nicolas Grollier.

ABOVE AND RIGHT: Depictions of the Platonic solids were common in this genre.

LATER GERMAN CONTRIBUTORS

Whatever the particular circumstances that gave rise to the short-lived genre of imaginative geometric fantasies it has qualities that make it unique in art, but by the end of the 16th century the vogue for geometric invention seems largely to have run its course. Geometric/Perspective treatises after this time still included geometric figures to demonstrate their theories, but in general they are far less adventurous. The volume by Paul Pfinzing, *Extract der Geometriae und Perspective*, is typical in this respect.

Pfinzing was born into a Nuremberg patrician family in 1554, and is best known as a cartographer, a field in which he was a pioneer. From around 1583 his print-shop produced a series of very highly regarded maps of Nuremberg, and in 1598 he published his geometric treatise in a limited edition 'for friends'. The intention of Pfinzing's book is more clearly didactic than those of the four previous artists. It refers to the geometry of the regular solids, and has a series of odd geometric constructs in association with the technical instruments used to produce perspective drawings of them. Although the overall effect is slightly incongruous, enough was thought of the book for it to be republished in 1616, after Pfinzing's death.

Thereafter, among German authors at least, the tradition of fanciful 'perspectival' geometry seems almost to have ended. There is however one last, intriguing, venture into this tradition. In 1625 the stonemason Peter Halt produced a book *Perspectivische Reiss Kunst* ('The Perspectival Art of Drawing', Augsburg) which was ostensibly aimed at craftsmen – stonemasons, carpenters, woodworkers etc. His drawings are clearly influenced by Lorenz Stoer, who he may have known personally. Much of the book is concerned with the construction of geometric figures, both on the plane and extended into three dimensions. Halt apparently used a 'Perspectograph' of his own devising as an aid to his drawings, a gadget that resembles the one made by Lucas Brunn (and it is likely that both devices were based on Jamnitzer's model), but he also emphasises the role of artistic imagination. On the theoretical side Halt offers a synthesis of Jamnitzer's Platonic notions of polyhedral forms as the basic 'building blocks' of reality with Lencker's emphasis on the alphabet. In this scheme the five vowels are identified with the five regular solids, which he proudly illustrates on his title-page. Using a somewhat contrived analogy, he explains that a familiarity with the basic regular polyhedra is as essential to the creation of three-dimensional forms (in any medium), in the same way that a knowledge of the vowels are essential to the comprehension of language – a conceit that is in complete accord with the Pythagorean/Platonic ideas of Jamnitzer and his followers. Peter Halt's drawings are not quite as confident or imaginative as Jamnitzer's, but they are very much in this tradition of fanciful geometry and have a certain originality of their own.

So, nearly sixty years after the publication of Jamnitzer's *Perspectiva Corporum Regularium*, and almost exactly a hundred years after Dürer's *Underweysung der Messung*, Peter Halt's work brings an end to this somewhat overlooked genre of geometricism in German art. In art-historical terms this style did indeed enjoy a brief flowering, but looking at these forms from the vantage of our postmodern present, it seems likely that their abstract, sculptural quality probably makes more artistic sense now than at any time since they were produced.

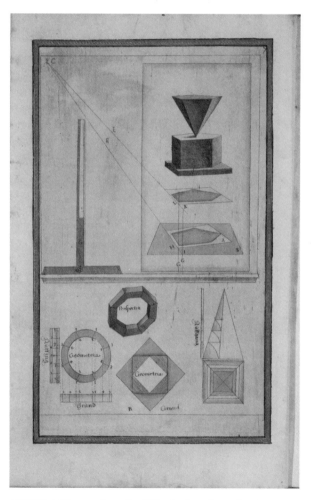

ABOVE: A Diagram from Paul Pfinzing's early production of *Extract der Geometriae und Perspective*, published in Nuremberg, 1598.

ABOVE: An inventive geometric figure from Peter Halt's *Perspectivische Reiss Kunst*, published in Augsburg, 162.

PAUL PFINZING

ABOVE: Paul Pfinzing (1554–1599).

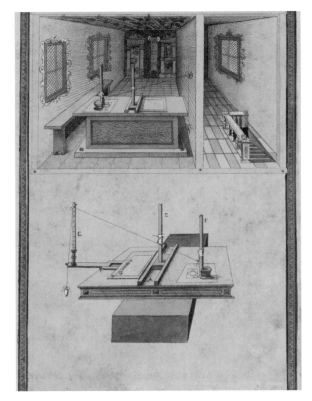

Pfinzing was a printer, publisher and cartographer who is most famous for producing a brilliant series of maps of Nuremberg and its environs in the 1580s. Cartography had become popular, almost a craze, during the 16th century, with gifted amateurs joining the ranks of professional surveyor/mapmakers; Pfinzing was a prime example of the former.

In 1598, towards the end of his life, he composed a somewhat fragmented geometric/perspective treatise in a limited edition, 'for friends'. This work was a more clearly didactic production than those of Jamnitzer and his immediate followers and presented various geometric constructs together with the tools of his other great passion, cartography – namely, instruments for drawing, measuring and surveying.

ABOVE: Paul Pfinzing's surveying/perspective table.

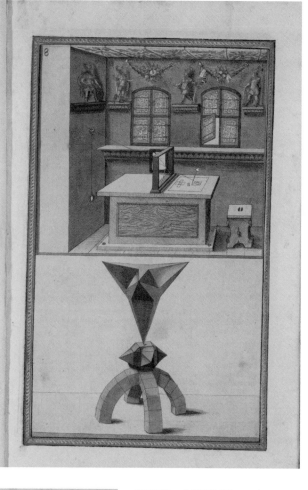

ALbrecht Dürer der Kunstreiche / hat in diesen Perspectiv sachen / soviel erfunden / daß er im Endt seines Buchs einen leichten vnnd geringen Weg Perspectivam auffzureissen anzeigt.

Ist also geschehen: Er setzt ihme ein geviertes Rohm / mit einem Thürlein / welches sich auff vnnd zu thun kan / auff einen Tisch / schraubt solches an / damit es nicht weichen kan / vnd dann hefft er mit Wachs an das Thürlein ein Bogen Pappir A.

Ferner reist er eine Geometriam auff / vnd legt solche hinder das Rohm nider B. vnnd hefft solche auch mit Wachs auff.

Nimbt alls dann ein lange Saiden / daran bindt er ein klein gewicht / vnnd am andern Endt / fast er einen Stefft an / vnnd macht ihm gegen dem Tisch ein schrauben inn die Wandt / daran legt er die Saiden / vnnd nimbt den Stefft / thut solchen durch das Rohm / vnnd setzt denselben auff einen Punct inn der Geometria / den er inn Perspectiv wissen vnnd haben will / left ihme solchen Stefft auff den Puncten vnuerruckt still halten.

Vnnd hat oben inn beyden Winckeln deß Rohms zwen lange seden / die schrenckt er kreutzweiß vbereinander / das die Saiden im kreutz eingefangen ist / dann hefft er die beyde seden mit Wachs an / daß sie vnuerruckt das kreutz behalten / vnd bleiben müssen / volgendt left er die Saiden zu ruck auß dem Rohm gehen / left als dann das Thürlein ins Rohm zugehen / vnnd sticht das kreutz am faden auff seinem Pappir ab / also findt er seinen Perspectiv Punct: Wann er nun den grunde inns Perspectiv gelegt hat / vnnd das Corpus auffziehen will / so hefft er die Saiden so viel höher an dem Stefft auff / vnnd handelt mit dem Auffzug gleich als zuvor. Da er nun die Puncten also hat / so hebt er das Thürlein ab / vnnd zeugt die Puncten mit geraden Linien zusammen / so find er das Corpus oder was er zu wercken vor hat.

ES bericht Albrecht Dürer noch ein Art Perspectivam auffzureissen / das ist / wie man auß dem Gesicht / durch ein Glaß von der Handt abzeichnen soll / es gehört aber allein vor diese / die in der Mahler Kunst schon Meister / vnnd von der Handt wol reissen vnnd stellen können.

Wen.

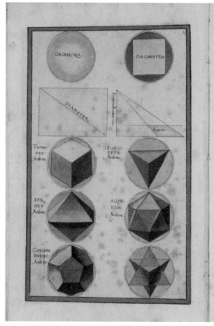

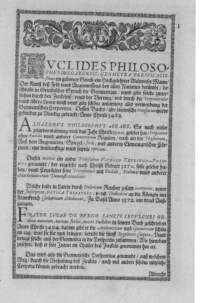

ABOVE and LEFT: Illustrations from Paul Pfinzing's early production of *Extract der Geometriae und Perspective*, Nuremberg 1598.

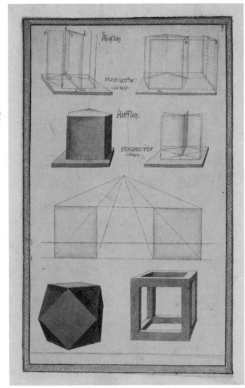

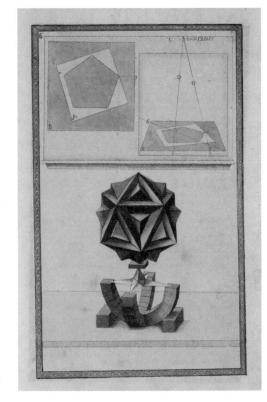

RIGHT & OPPOSITE LEFT: Illustrations from Paul Pfinzing's posthumously-published *Extract der Geometriae und Perspective*, featuring the technical instruments he used in surveying and the production of perspective drawings.

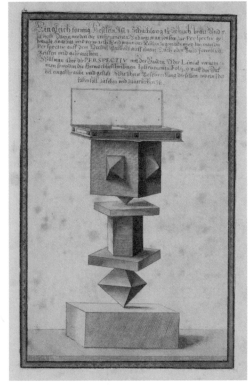

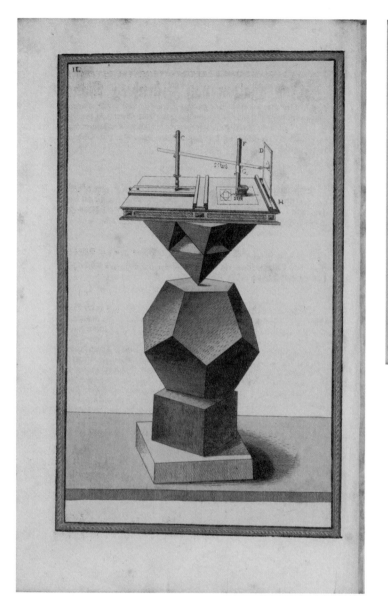

Pfinzing's approach to cartography was innovative and highly practical. He devised pedometers to be used by assistants on foot and by horse and wagon, to accurately determine the distance travelled on his many surveying missions. The outcome of his labours in the field were printed in his own print-shop in Nuremberg, in the form of a magnificent twenty-eight page Atlas of the Nuremberg Region, containing some thirty-four beautifully illustrated maps – which he presented to his home town in 1594. This is now rightly regarded as an antiquarian classic.

ABOVE: Pfinzing was a printer and publisher, most famous for producing a brilliant series of maps of Nuremberg and its environs in the 1580s. As a cartographer he was innovative and highly practical, a gifted amateur. This drawing shows him at work at his drafting table: from his *Extract der Geometriae und Perspective*,1598.

PETER HALT (fl.1629–1653)

ABOVE: Peter Halt's enthusiasm and inventiveness are evident in the sheer number of drawings he produced in this genre – his *Perspectivische Reiss Kunst*, published in Augsburg in 1625, has more than 170 figures.

Little is known of this artist/craftsman other than that he was a stonemason by trade, and practised as an architect in Schorndorf. The *Perspectivische Reiss Kunst*, his only book in this genre, was clearly influenced by Jamnitzer. He may have also have known Lorenz Stoer personally, since both were in Augsburg in the early 1600s. In 1626 Halt produced a rather strange booklet, *Drei Wichtige newe Kuntststuck in underschidlichen Perspectivischen Instrumentum inventiert und erfunden*, which contained little more than a detailed description of two drawing devices of his own making.

His *Perspectivische Reiss Kunst* is a veritable *tour de force* of Geometricism, containing some 170 drawings of geometric figures. Many of these are similar to those produced by Jamnitzer, Stoer and Lencker, and he follows Jamnitzer in his proposal of a scheme equating the five regular Platonic solids with the five vowels, but within this somewhat restricted genre he displays a distinct originality. If he actually transcribed any of artistic inventions his into stone they have unfortunately not survived.

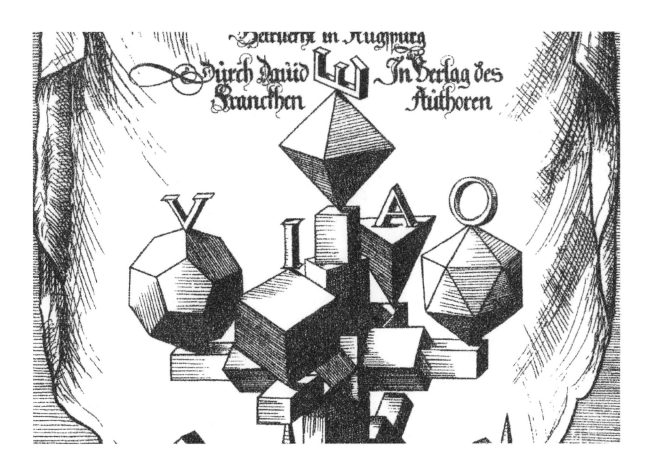

TOP: Detail of the title-page of Peter Halt's
Perspectivische Reiss Kunst, (Augsburg, 1625), in
which he clearly identifies the five regular 'Platonic'
solids with the five vowels.

ABOVE: Two variants of conical figures, clearly owing
a great deal to Wenzel Jamnitzer

TOP & OPPOSITE: *Mazzocchio* figures from Halt's *Perspectivische Reiss Kunst*

BOTTOM: Although very much in the tradition going back to Leonardo, Peter Halt manages to infuse some of his own originality into these polyhedral models

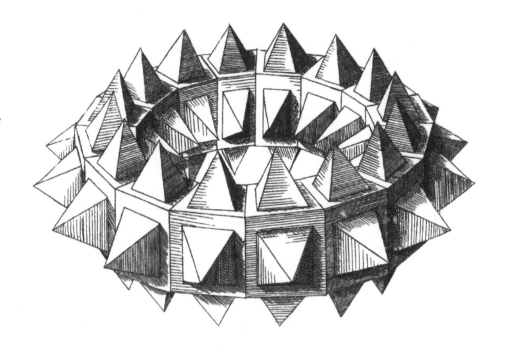

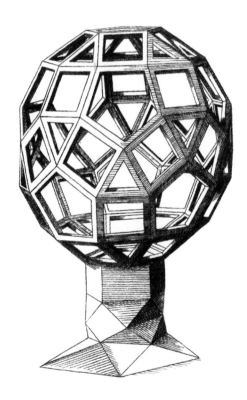

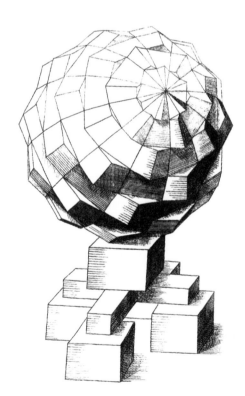

BOTTOM: Further examples of the imaginative drawings by the stonemason Peter Halt; from his *Perspectivische Reiss Kunst* (Augsburg, 1625)

PETER HALT   183

JOHANNES KEPLER: CELESTIAL MATHEMATICIAN

Johannes Kepler (1571–1630) was born in modest circumstances, in a small town in Swabia, Southern Germany. Another brilliant and precocious talent, his aptitude for mathematics was first realised at his local school, which led to his acceptance into a seminary, and eventually to the University at Tubingen. At Tubingen Kepler first encountered the extraordinarily radical Copernican model of a sun-centred planetary system, which he rapidly accepted.

His life-long mission thereafter was to investigate the physical nature of the planets, their relationship to each other, and of the mathematical character of their orbits around the Sun. His first ideas on this extraordinarily ambitious project were published in the *Mysterium Cosmographicum* ('The Mystery of The Cosmos', 1596). Written in his early twenties, it is now famous as the first published assertion of the Copernican

ABOVE: Johannes Kepler (1571–1630).

heliocentric theory. In this Kepler proposed a geometric scheme for the orbits of the six (then known) planets. He was influenced throughout his career by the Platonic notion that an archetypal world of forms and ideas lay behind the world of physical appearances. These ideas, combined with his commitment to Protestant theology, led him to the belief that geometry was 'co-eternal with the divine mind'. In the *Mysterium* he lays out what he believed to be the order of this divine geometry.

Kepler's first attempts at uncovering a geometric schema to account for the observable orbits of the planets involved various arrangements of polygons within circumscribing circles. When this attempt proved unsatisfactory he turned to arrangements of 'nested' polyhedra, i.e. one within another, to find a convincing model of the geometry underlying the Universe – but ultimately the data could not be made

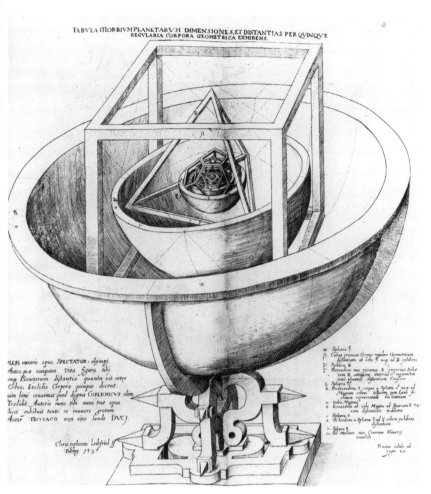

PLERI mirari opus. SPECTATOR. olympi.
Antea qua nunquam Vrta figura tibi
sunt Planetarum distantia quanta sit inter
Orbes Euclidis Corpora quinque docent.
nam bene conuenuat quod dogma COPERNICVS olim
Tradidit. Autoris nunc tibi moni trat opus
licet exhibuit tanto se munere gratum
Autor TECCIACO non sine laude DVCJ.

Chris tophorus Leibfried ff
Tubing 1597

Picture tabula ad
page 26.

α Sphera ♄.
β. Cubus primum Corpus regulare Geometricum
distantiam ab orbe ♄ usq; ad ♃ exhibens
γ. Sphera ♃.
V. Tetraedron siue pyramis. 3. exterius Schema ♃ attingens, interiori & inequentium
inter planetas distantium Confinio
δ. Sphera ♂.
ε. Dodecaedron, ♀ corpus a Sphera ♂ usq; ad
Magnum orbem tellurym cum Luna sic
redeum repraesentans dut tantum
ζ. Orbis Magnus.
θ. Icosaedron ab orbe Magno ad Sphaeram ♀ 24:
ram distantiam in dicans
ι. Sphera ♀.
x. Octaedron à Sphera ♀ ad V orbem exhibens
distantiam
λ. Sphera ☿.
μ. Sol Medium mar, Centrum Vniuersi
immobile.

Johannes Kepler's search for the relationships between planetary orbits led him to investigate cosmological schemes based on Plato's five regular solids. He made many attempts at fitting the observed planetary data into various combinations of 'nested' regular polyhedra. In his final scheme, **LEFT:** Kepler placed an octahedron between the orbits of Mercury and Venus, an icosahedron between Venus and Earth, a dodecahedron between Earth and Mars, a tetrahedron between Mars and Jupiter, and a cube between Jupiter and Saturn.
ABOVE: shows a close-up of the inner section of this scheme. This cosmological arrangement was presented in his *Mysterium Cosmographicum* of 1596 (see over).

to fit the theory, and this imaginative scheme also failed.

In 1610 Galileo published his discovery of Jupiter's moons, an event that greatly impressed Kepler and inspired him in his own study of the properties of lenses (published as *Dioptrice*, 1611), in which he presented his idea for a more advanced type of telescope using two convex lenses; this proved to be an entirely successful design that soon gained universal acceptance. Also in 1611 Kepler produced a charming essay 'On Hexagonal Snow', (*Strena seu de Niva Sexangula*), in which a meditation on the hexagonal symmetry of snow-crystals lead him to consider different arrangements of two- and three-dimensional close packing, both in Nature

and in mathematical theory. Out of this came an explanation of the structure of honeybee-cells and the speculation that a hexagonal arrangement of spheres would fill space in the most efficient way – a conjecture that, surprisingly, had to wait till the 21st century for verification.

Of particular relevance in this context, Kepler made a systematic study of polyhedra, placing them into classes for the first time, and proving that these classes were complete – he was the first to do this for the thirteen convex uniform polyhedra (the so-called Archimedean solids). Two important polyhedra, the small stellated dodecahedron and the great stellated dodecahedron, bear his name (although they had actually been depicted previously by both Uccello and Jamnitzer) and he gave them a mathematical description, realising that, technically speaking, they were *regular* polyhedra. He also discovered the rhombic dodecahedron and rhombic triacontrahedron.

Kepler was truly modern and a true scientist. He was inspired by an ideal Platonic vision, and never entirely abandoned the idea of an orderly Universe. But although he continued to search for geometrical and numerological relationships among the planets and elsewhere, in the end these were only acceptable if they conformed to the observable phenomena. In his *Harmonices Mundi* ('The Harmony of the World', 1619), he finally presented his laws of planetary motion (which still stand); at the age of fifty, he returned to the *Mysterium*, publishing a greatly extended version in 1621.

Kepler was another to whom the expression 'last of the magicians, first of scientists' applies;

he was a visionary, but a very practical one. Always guided by Platonic notions of a perfectly structured, geometrically harmonic universe, he pursued this path to an almost obsessive degree. His mathematics placed the Copernican heliocentric theory on an unassailable footing, and through this work alone he really did open doors to our greater, modern understanding of the workings of the Universe.

It is worth remembering however, that although the Renaissance is associated with the rise of Humanism, this period was also the heyday of the European witch-craze. Kepler's mother was a victim of this hysterical movement, and was only saved from burning at the stake through Kepler's energetic efforts in her defence.

THE STRENA

On New Year's Day, 1611 Kepler presented a group of his friends with a short but delightful essay on 'The Six-Cornered Snowflake' (*Strena seu de Nive Sexangula*), a work that investigated geometry in Nature. He reflects on such formations as the hexagonal structure of the bee's cell, the rhombohedral packing of pomegranate seeds, the geometry of crystal forms and the delicate symmetries of snowflakes themselves. He also touches on the purely mathematical problems involved in the regular division of space – the regular distribution of circles on the plane and of spheres in three-dimensions. Kepler was fully conversant with the ideas of the Pythagoreans and was sympathetic to their idea that the ultimate truths of reality and the highest

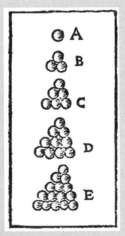

ABOVE: Diagram from *Strena seu de Nive Sexangula*, 1611, in which Kepler investigates the close close-packing of spheres and relates this to the formation of crystals, including the six-sided snowflake.

aesthetic qualities were in some way contained in number and geometry. His life-long project was to uncover just such a set of all-embracing, divine principles as they proposed – 'Why waste words. Geometry existed before the Creation, is co-eternal with the mind of God. Is God himself'.

In the event however, Kepler did not pursue the line of enquiry that he laid out in his essay and the intuition that led him to associate the geometry of close-packing with the structure of crystals was not followed up. His instincts in this direction were on the right track, but his genius was destined to reveal the mysteries of the macro- rather than the micro-world.

THE POLYHEDRAL COSMOLOGY

Both of the important 16th century astronomers Tycho Brahe and Johannes Kepler are known to have possessed copies of Jamnitzer's *Perspectiva Corporum Regularium*, and both were very taken with the cosmological notions that it expressed. Kepler, in particular, was inspired by these ideas in the formation of his own speculations on the structure of the universe. He made a systematic study of the Platonic and Archimedean solids, and attempted to relate their volumetric ratios to distances of the planets from the Sun. His discovery that each of the Platonic solids could be inscribed and circumscribed within spheres, led to the famous model of 'nested' polyhedra as a representation of the ratios of planetary orbits.

In his *Mysterium Cosmographicum* 1596 Kepler attempted to account for the relationships between the planetary orbits in Classical geometric terms. In this book he stated his intention to show that 'the most great and good Creator, in this creation of the moving universe and the arrangements of the heavens, looked to the five regular solids, which have been so celebrated from the time of Pythagoras and Plato down to our own, and that he fitted to the nature of those solids the number of the heavens, their

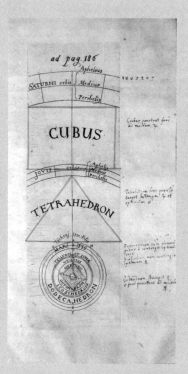

proportions and the law of their motion.'

In this scheme Kepler placed an octahedron between the orbits of Mercury and Venus, an icosahedron between Venus and Earth, a dodecahedron between Earth and Mars, a tetrahedron between Mars and Jupiter, and a cube between Jupiter and Saturn. At this stage in his career Kepler was so convinced that he had discovered the basis of a celestial harmony that he pursued the idea of developing this model into a 'cosmic bowl' that would dispense beverages appropriate

LEFT: Kepler's life-long mission was to investigate the physical and mathematical character of the planets motion around the Sun. His first ideas on this were based on a series of regular polygons inscribed within their orbits.

to the symmetries of the various polyhedra and the planets that they represented – but the scheme was never realised. Although he later rejected his nested polyhedral model, the astronomical work for which he became famous (his Three Laws of planetary motion) was essentially a further development of these ideas.

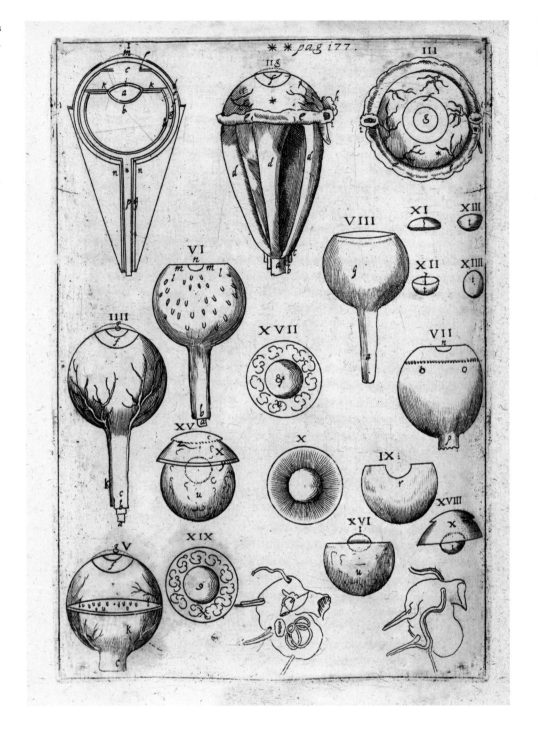

HARMONICES MUNDI

In 1619 Kepler published his 'Harmony of the World' (*Harmonices Mundi*), a book that is very Pythagorean/Platonic in tone, which deals with the symmetries and harmonies of geometrical figures and other physical phenomena. It is most famous today for its almost casual announcement at the end of the book of his Third Law of Planetary Motion.

Kepler firmly believed that the secret of universal order could be found in geometry, that 'Geometry was co-eternal with the divine mind'. The book begins with an investigation into plane and polyhedral geometry, and reiterates the Platonic identification of the five regular solids with the four basic Elements plus the Cosmos. On a more conventional note it ranks polyhedra according to their regularity and semi-regularity, and shows their relative degrees of congruence including the ways in which they are able to form duals. It also provides the first mathematical description of the small stellated polyhedron and the great stellated dodecahedron.

In the *Harmonices* Kepler examines the harmonic relations between the volumes of various solids, of the principles of consonance in music, and of the

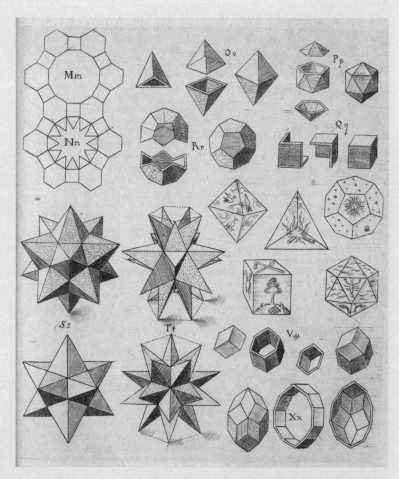

relative spacings between planets in the Solar System. He regarded it as his greatest book; 'I may say with truth that whenever I consider in my thoughts the beautiful order, how one thing issues out of, and is derived from another, then it is as though I had read a divine text, written into the world itself, not with letters but rather with essential objects'.

ABOVE: Kepler's investigations into polyhedral geometry, showing the Platonic identification of the five regular solids with the four basic Elements plus the Cosmos; he also describes here the small stellated polyhedron. Kepler firmly believed that the secret of universal order could be found in geometry, that 'Geometry was co-eternal with the divine mind'. From the *Harmonices Mundi*, 1619.

GEOMETRIC MOTIFS IN GERMAN *INTARSIA*

During the Northern Renaissance *Intarsia*, together with its associated geometrical motifs and the use of *trompe l'oeil* spread to Germany, to such centres as Nuremberg and Augsburg, where it became extremely popular – indeed, for a while it was almost a mania (*intarsienmanie*). German *intarsia* began in the south, taking root in the towns where furniture-making was well established, Augsburg and Nuremberg. The earlier examples, in common with the Italian tradition, seem to have been made by monks as decoration for Church furniture, but little has survived of this work. By the mid-16th century the religious upheavals affecting this part of Germany meant that commissions from the Church dried up, and later *intarsia* is clearly intended for domestic interiors and has no religious connotations. German *intarsia* craftsmen usually worked from drawings by artists, but they, like their Italian counterparts, also borrowed from prints. Exotic woods and ivory were widely used, and towards the end of the 16th century the invention of a fast-moving frame-held jigsaw greatly facilitated production. The form did however go out of fashion, as in Italy.

German *intarsia* shows less interest in perspective than the Italian examples, and there is a predominance of flat patterns. A great deal of this work, it has to be said, is rather tasteless, but these examples, which use a geometrical theme, (which is particularly suited to *intarsia*), have an engaging, quite modernistic, quality of their own.

ABOVE: *Cover of intarsia* writing desk, Ausburg, 16th century

ABOVE: Large Kabinett with many panels and drawers in Intarsia, Nuremberg, 16th century.

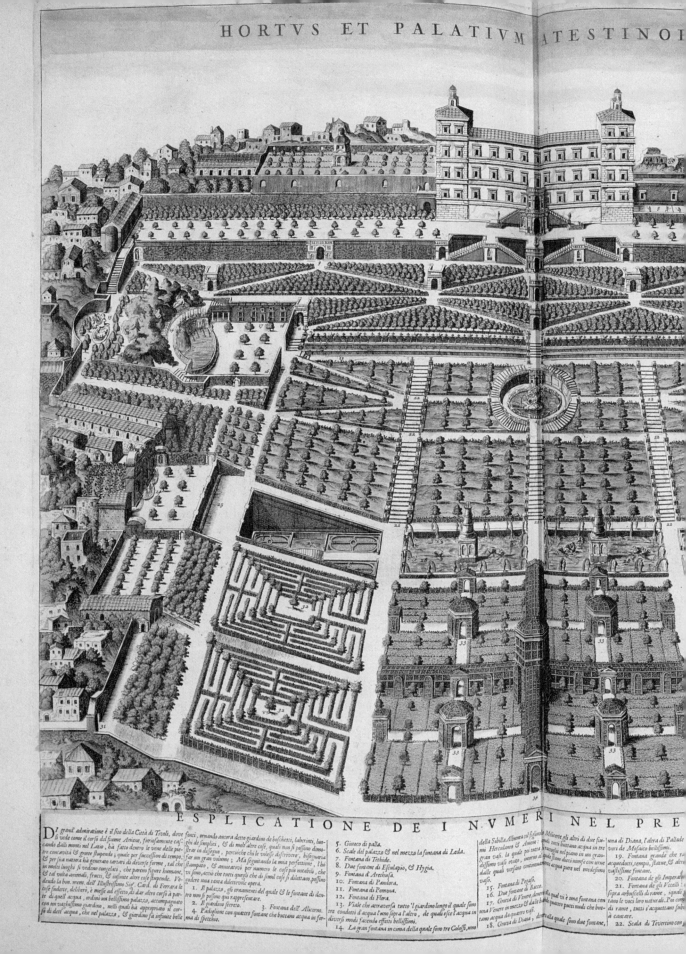

Di gran admiratione è il sito della Città di Tivoli, dove si vede come il corso del fiume Aniene, furiosamente cascando dalli monti il Latio, hà fatto dentro le vene delle pietre concavità & grotte stupende; quale per succession di tempo, & per sua natura hà generato tartari di diverse forme, tal che in molti luoghi fi vedono congelati, che pareno figure humane, & tal volta animali, frutti, & infinite cose stupende. Vedendo la bon. mem. dell'Illustrissimo Sig.r Card. di Ferrara le cose sudette, deliberò, & messe ad effetto di dar altro corso à parte di quell'acqua, ordinò un bellissimo palazzo, accompagnato con vaghissimo giardino, nelli quali hà appropriato il corso di detti acqua, che nel palazzo, & giardino fà infinite belle fonti, ornando ancora detto giardino de boschetti, laberinti, luoghi de simplici, & di mol'altre cose, quali non si possono domostrar in difegno, perciòche chi le volesse descrivere, bisogneria far un gran volume; Ma seguitando la mia perfettione, l'hò stampato, & annotatovi per numero le cose più notabili, che vi sono, accio che tutti quelli che di simil cose si dilettano possino godere una tanta dilettevole opera.

5. Giuoco di palla.
6. Scale del palazzo & nel mezzo la fontana di Leda.
7. Fontana di Tethide.
8. Due fontane di Esculapio, & Hygia.
9. Fontana d'Arethusa.
10. Fontana di Pandora.
11. Fontana di Pomona.
12. Fontana di Flora.
13. Viale che attraversa tutto 'l giardino lungo il quale sono tre condotti d'acqua l'uno sopra l'altro, de quali esce l'acqua in diversi modi facendo effetti bellissimi.
14. La gran fontana in cima della quale sono tre Colossi, uno

1. Il palazzo, gli ornamenti del quale & le fontane di dentro non si possono qui rappresentare.
2. Il giardino secreto.
3. Fontana dell'Alicorno.
4. Padiglioni con quattro fontane che buttano acqua in forma di specchio.

della Sibilla Albunea col giovane Melicerte gli altri di due fiumi Hercolano & Aniene: tutti buttano acqua in un grandissimo vaso, la quale poi cascando nel piano in un grandissimo vaso evivo, ascende di quello stano dieci ninfe con urne dalle quali versano continuamente acqua pare nel medesimo vaso.
15. Fontana di Pegaso.
16. Due fontane di Bacco.
17. Grotta di Venere, dove la qual vi è una fontana di Venere in mezzo & dalle quattro putti nudi che buttano acqua da quattro vasi.
18. Grotta di Diana, dentro alla quale sono due fontane

19. Fontana grande che sù acquedotti, tempi, statue, & altre vastissime fontane.
20. Fontana de gli Imperatori.
21. Fontana de gli Vccelli, sopra arboscelli di rame, i quali buttano le voci loro naturali. Poi con un'altra mutatione si sente un Gufo, che tutti s'acquetano di cantare.
22. Scala di Tevertino con

una di Diana, l'altra di Pallade vere de Mosaico bellissimi.

DISEGNO:

...spra ciafcbiadono de quali efce un capo d'acqua in...
...tore.
...tana de draghi von un capo d'acqua, la quale fa-
...omo, nell'ufcire fa ftrepiti come colps d'artigliaria.
...tana della Dea della natura. Quefta fontana
...si pus chiamare dalle merauiglie.Entri uno organo
...murabile artificio a forza d'acqua fuona da fe fteffo
...ale ò mettere che fi voglia à quattro, o cinque voci.
...cofe affai pin ftupende vi hanno da effere , ma non
...a.
...ntte delle Sibille.
...tana d'Antenore.

27. *Pefchiere fatte à patrimenti.*
28. *Pefchiere von mota fudante nel meffe.*
29. *Fontana di Nettuno che rapprefenta il Mare oceano.*
30. *Fontana di Venere Claucnia.*
31. *Fontana di Tritone.*
32. *Laberinti.*
33. *Giardino delli Semplici.*
34. *Intrata del giardino che non è fopra il diffegno con cer-*
    chiate & due fontane ruftiche.
35. *Loghetti fuori del giardino.*

V

THE CONTINUING INFLUENCE *of* GEOMETRIA

From the mid-17ᵗʰ century on, the taste for Geometry as a mode of artistic expression decreased, but this was a gradual process and traces of geometricism survived in the decorative arts, notably in garden design; geometrical and perspective studies were absorbed into formal mathematics. However, during this same period, three-dimensional geometry began to assume an important new role in the emerging science of Crystallography.

LEFT: The magnificent geometric formality of the Renaissance garden: Étiennes Dupérac's birds-eye view of the gardens of the *Villa d'Este*, on the western slope of the town of Tivoli in the Lazio region, constructed by Pirro Ligorio (c. 1500–1583) This print was itself highly influential in spreading ideas of the formal Renaissance garden to Northern Europe.

LATER GEOMETRIC / PERSPECTIVE TREATISES IN ITALY

Artistic influences flowed freely during the Renaissance; aesthetic tastes and technical developments that originated on one side of the Alps were, sooner or later, taken across to the other – and these influences tended to follow long-established trade routes. Venice, whose merchants had been operating there since the 1300s, had close commercial and cultural ties with Nuremberg. It was therefore quite natural that book production, which had originated and flourished in Nuremberg, should have established itself earlier and more successfully in Venice than elsewhere in Italy. Even as early as the 1500s there were dozens of Nuremberg printers working in Venice, producing books on all manner of topics. However, Italian authors were slower than their German counterparts in the field of perspective theory. After Luca Pacioli and Leonardo's *De Divina Proportione* in 1509, no Italian works on this subject using three-dimensional regular figures appeared until Daniel Barbaro's *La Pratica della Perspettiva* in 1569.

Daniel Barbaro (1513–1570) was an aristocratic philosopher and mathematician, most famous for his translation and commentary of Vitruvius (for which his friend Andrea Palladio provided the illustrations, see pages 98/101). His perspective book attempts a thorough, comprehensive account of the subject, dealing with each of various aspects that had been covered by earlier German theorists – including a substantial section on the regular and semi-regular solids for which he provides 'nets' and perspective views. He includes descriptions and drawings of some stellated figures, and the stock Geometric/Perspective treatise item of a *mazzocchio*, plus variants. Barbaro's book is serious and didactic in tone, with an emphasis on mathematical explanations, but he does allow himself one flight of geometric fantasy with a curious armoured sphere, possibly inspired by a drawing by Uccello.

After this, interest seems again to have waned; geometrical bodies did not appear in print form in Italy until nearly thirty years later, with Lorenzo Sirigatti's (1596–1625) *La Pratica di Prospettiva* ('The Practice of Perspective', Venice, 1596). Sirigatti's book, particularly by contrast with Barbaro's, is light on the theory of perspective but presents a series of finely drawn solid and 'skeletised' regular figures, plus a number of intriguing variations of spherical bodies and *mazzocchio*. Many of these latter figures have the same spiky, armoured appearance as Barbaro's sphere. Sirigatti ends his collection with two assemblages of geometric shapes, very much in the style of Jamnitzer and Stoer, but these are almost the final throw of the sub-genre of fantastic geometry in Italy.

Pietro Accolti (1570–1642), who was also an architect, did use geometrical figures in his *Prospettiva Pratica* ('Practical Perspective', Florence, 1625), but this workmanlike production is heavy on theory and the illustrations are purely of didactic interest. Mario Bettini (1582–1657), an Italian Jesuit philosopher, mathematician and astronomer was responsible for several important mathematical works, including *Aerarium Philosophiae Mathematicae*, ('A Treasury of Mathematical Philosophy', Rome, 1648), which is essentially an encyclopaedia of mathematical curiosities. In this, various regular figures and their nets are presented in an attractive format, but again, the intention is purely didactic.

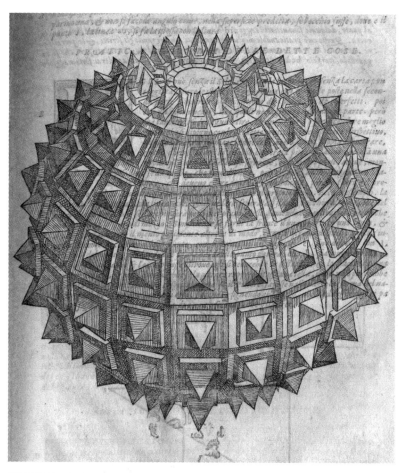

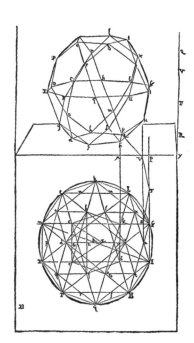

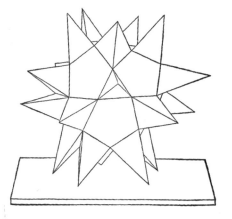

ABOVE: Polyhedra and a stellated spherical figure, reminiscent of a drawing by Uccello. From Danielle Barbaro's *La Practica della Perspettiva*, Venice, 1569. A Venetian aristocrat, diplomat and cardinal, Barbaro is best known for his translation of the ten books of Vitruvius, *De Architectura* (for which Palladio provided the illustrations).

BELOW AND RIGHT: Pages from Lorenzo Sirigatti's *La Practica di Prospettiva*, Venice, 1596.

Sirigatti was a Florentine mathematician who is known to have lectured in Bologna. His work on perspective was very popular, running to 11 editions. However, like Jamnitzer's and Lencker's works, it is not really explanatory – although it impressed Galileo who is reputed to have seen it pre-publication. It is possible that Sirigatti's convincing images of shaded spheres inspired Galileo's drawings of the surface of the moon. Although there is little biographical detail, he is believed to have been appointed as a Bishop by Pope Sixtus Quintus 'for his many praise-worthy accomplishments'.

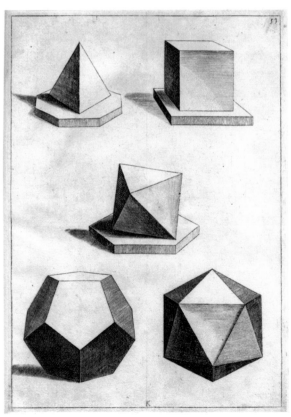

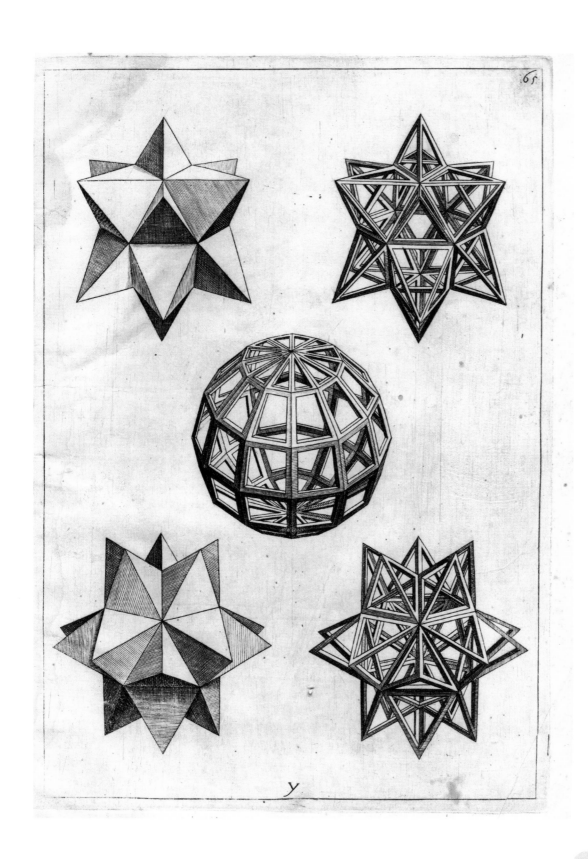

y

BELOW: From an engraved print, possibly by Martino da Udine (1470–1548).

The source, and artistic intention, of this strange drawing, which bear the monograph 'P.P.', is obscure. It has an affinity with certain sketches by Uccello, Barbaro and Leonardo, and clearly demonstrate a competence and familiarity with the rules of perspective, but otherwise little is known about it. It has been suggested (by Arthur M. Hind) that the monogram 'P.P.' is that of Martino da Udine, who according to the art-historian Georg K. Nagler worked in Ferrara and Udine. If so, other similar examples of this artists work have not survived, or have yet to be discovered.

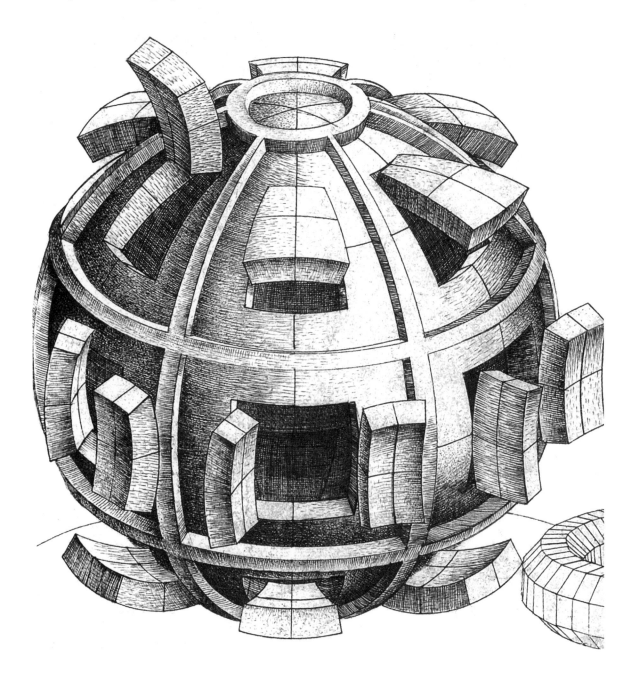

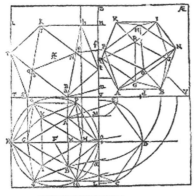

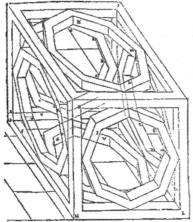

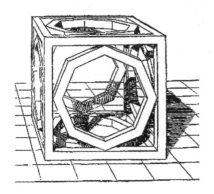

ABOVE: Drawings from Pietro Accolti's *Prospettiva Pratica*, Florence, 1625.

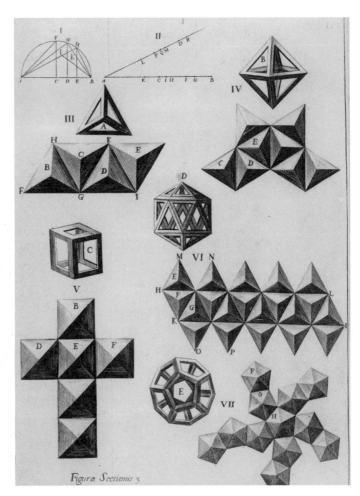

ABOVE: A page from Mario Bettini's *Aerarium Philosophiae Mathematicae*, 1648, showing nets of polyhedra. Bettini was an influential Jesuit philosopher, mathematician and astronomer.

LATER GEOMETRIC/PERSPECTIVE TREATISES IN ITALY

THE *MAZZOCCHIO*

The *Mazzocchio* was originally a hat, based on medieval originals, which became popular in Florence in the mid-15th century. This extravagant fashion item, or rather its supporting wicker-work frame, because of its complicated toroidal structure was adopted as a stock subject in Geometric/ Perspective Treatises. It was the only non-classical geometric form to be used for this purpose.

Uccello painted several versions of the Florentine hat itself in both *The Flood and Waters Subsiding* and the three panels of *The Battle of San Romano* (where it is worn by the central figure, Niccolò da Mauruzi da Tolentino); Leonardo da Vinci made several drawings of this object in his notebooks, and it also features in Wentzel Jamnitzer's and Johannes Lencker's books. Danielle Barbaro presents a series of variants in his perspective treatise, as does Lorenzo Sirigatti in his *Pratica della perspettiva*.

ABOVE RIGHT: The *Mazzocchio* as a signature detail in Uccello's paintings.

RIGHT: *Mazzocchio* figures from Danielle Barbaro's 'La Pratica della Perpectiva', Venice, 1569.

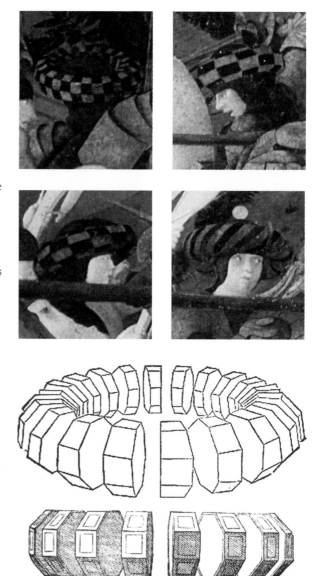

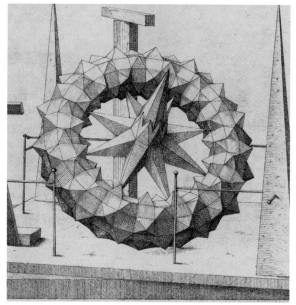

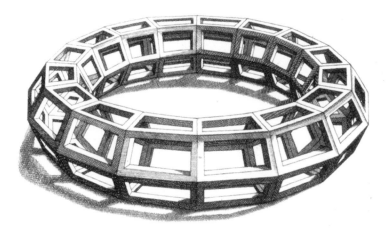

TOP: Leonardo da Vinci's elaborate drawing of a *Mazzocchio*; from his 'Atlantico' Codex sketchbook

CENTRE: Two stellated variations of a *Mazzocchio* by Wenzel Jamnitzer; from his 'Perspectiva Corporum Regularium', Nuremberg, 1568

LEFT: Lorenzo Sirigatti's version of a *Mazzocchio*; from 'La Practica di Prospettiva', Venice, 1596.

THE *MAZZOCHIO* 201

ESOTERIC, ARCANE & OCCULT GEOMETRIES

The perception that the Renaissance, with its Humanist agenda of civic and spiritual renewal, shook off medieval superstition in favour of a revival of the more rational philosophies of Classical Antiquity has some basis – but there was another aspect to this narrative (which was in any case something of a self-created myth). The Greek Classics were not the only manuscripts to be translated in Marsilio Ficino's Florentine Academy. The *Corpus Hermetica*, a compendium that included

texts on magic, astrology and alchemy, which were taken to be of Ancient Egyptian origin, were also translated into Latin by Ficino and given the same degree of respect as the Classical works of the Greek philosophers. Indeed, in the minds of many of the followers of the Academy these documents were of equal authority with those of Plato and Aristotle, and possibly of even greater antiquity.

In reality, the Hermetic literature was a jumbled collection of teachings (only parts of which derived

ABOVE: Abraham von Franckenberg's *Rafael albo Aniol-Lekarz* ('The Arch-angel Raphael or Angel-Doctor'), 1639. Frankenberg was a Silesian physician and poet. He was a supporter of the mystic Jakob Böhme and formed a Gnostic and Rosicrician movement.

LEFT AND ABOVE: Two of John Dee's magical seals. Dee was a renowned Elizabethan scholar, a mathematician and astronomer (and a confidant of Queen Elizabeth I) – but he was also steeped in Hermetic magic and Marsilio Ficino's version of Neo-Platonism, and did not distinguish between these disciplines.

from ancient sources), that were put together in the Hellenistic world of the 2ⁿᵈ–3ʳᵈ centuries AD. The collection of small books that comprised the *Corpus* was accepted as the revelations of the sage Hermes Trismegistus,* but in fact these dialogues encompass a wide range of beliefs, not all consistent, that range from the elevated and spiritual to the occult and magical. However, the *Hermetica* were accepted as genuine in their entirety by Marsilio Ficino and his Platonic Academy, and through this channel they entered the perfervid world of European occultism. This is all more comprehensible when we realise that Marsilio Ficino's Platonic Academy saw itself as an essentially elitist, secretive group that had chosen to engage with esoteric knowledge, many aspects of which the Church regarded as completely heretical, if nor positively Satanic. After all, had not St Augustine himself described the exploration of nature as the 'disease of curiosity'.

The philosophical and religious disparities between the various newly acquired texts and those of Church-approved Aristotolianism meant that the ideas of the former were sometimes bundled together, in an unlikely alliance of ideas. Thus, the rise of scientific curiosity from the mid-15ᵗʰ century was paralleled by a rise of interest in magic and the occult. As a result, the 'exploration of Nature', what we now recognise as the scientific enterprise, was, in its Renaissance infancy completely shot through with notions that were drawn from pagan mystery-religions. Many of its leading protagonists (Paracelsus, Agrippa, John Dee, Giordano Bruno), were as involved in arcane and occult studies as they were in science in the modern sense. Interestingly, many of these figures used geometric diagrams in their dissertations, which seemed to provide an authenticating gloss.

The 'Hermetic Tradition', from the time of its translation in Florence, was a source of inspiration for most European occult secret societies, including the Masonic and Rosicrucian movements.

* The original meaning of Trismegistus, 'the thrice-great', or 'thrice-blessed', is obscure, but it came to refer to the practices of Alchemy, Astrology and Theurgy (White magic).

ABOVE: A sculpture of two entangled tetrahedral, with seven smaller tetrahedral at their junctions. From the Church at St. Trivier de Courtes, region of Bourgogne, Eastern France.

ABOVE: An alabaster sculpture, featuring all the Platonic solids, that was presented to the Bodleian Library in 1620 by Sir Clement Edmonds, Fellow of All Souls.

ABOVE: Model of a truncated octahedron on the tomb of Sir Anthony Ashley in the parish Church of St, Giles near Salisbury, England.

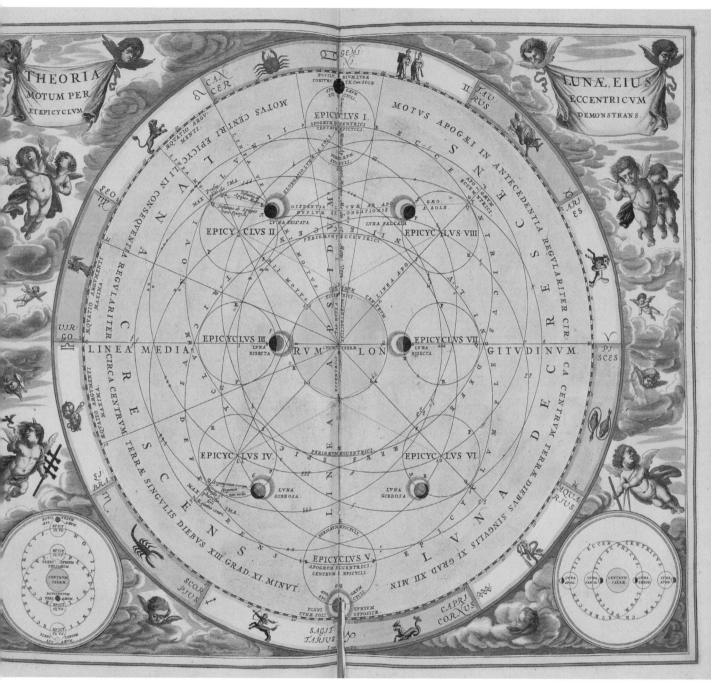

ABOVE: Andreas Cellarius's *Theoria Lunae Eius Motum per Eccentricum et Epicyclum Demonstrans*, showing the Moon's eccentric, epicyclic orbit – with Astrological references.

THE MAGICIAN/SCIENTISTS

'Magic comprises the most profound contemplation of the most sacred things, their nature, power, quality, substance and virtues, as well as the knowledge of their whole nature.' Heinrich Cornelius Agrippa (1486–1494), *De Occulta Philosophia*.

After the Reformation and the breakdown of the Catholic Church's hegemony in the early 16th century a number of arcane, supposedly secret, traditions, appeared to fill the spiritual gap. These 'secret traditions', the Hermetic and others that followed (notably, the Rosicrucians in the 17th century, and the Freemasons in the 18th), were viewed by the Church as rival theologies. Ficino himself had faced serious opposition from the Church, was accused of practicing magic, and had attracted the attention of the Roman Inquisition. He was fortunate enough to enjoy the protection of his powerful patrons, the Medicis. Even so, his Academy had to dissimulate and disguise its aims and identity. Ficino managed to stay out of trouble, but his pupil, Pico della Mirandola, was not so lucky. Mirandola attempted a synthesis of all known systems of philosophy and religion (including the Hermetic tradition), but his ideas were condemned by the Pope and he had to flee to France. In the course of the 16th century the

Church became ever more hostile towards scientific/magical ideas, culminating in the trial of the philosopher and mathematician Giordano Bruno on charges of blasphemy and heresy. Bruno had flaunted both his pantheism and his belief in the Sun-centred Copernican cosmology, and refused to recant either. For this he was burnt at the stake.

The dangers were less intense further away from the reaches of the Catholic Church and its Inquisition. The German philosopher Heinrich Cornelius Agrippa was a self-avowed magician and alchemist who came under suspicion of involvement in black magic, but who saw himself as a Christian reformer. He was part of the Humanist tradition that included Marsilio Ficino and Desiderius Erasmus, and was in turn a major influence on such thinkers as Giordano Bruno and John Dee. Agrippa's near contemporary, the Swiss-German Paracelsus (Philippus Aureolus Theophrastus Bombastus von Hohenheim) was an important pioneer of diagnostic medicine. He too was an occultist, but was also radical in his insistence on observing nature rather than depending on accepted texts in the Scholastic manner.

Although an interest in the arcane and occult did give offence to the Church, there was little sense of

ABOVE, CENTRE AND RIGHT: Woodcuts of magical figures (of uncertain meaning), from Giordano Bruno's *Articuli Centum et Sexaginta*

Adversus Huius Tempestatis Mathematicus atque Philososophus, published in Prague in 1588, two years before his fatal return to Italy.

sensationalism among its practitioners; it was merely another path of investigation of the natural world. Gerolamo Cardano, for instance, is best known these days as a pioneer of algebra and probabilistic mathematics, but in his own time he was a renowned physician and occultist. The mathematician/philosopher Giambattista Della Porta founded a scientific club that was forced to close after accusations of dealing with occult matters. He was summoned to Rome on this account, to explain himself to the Roman Inquisition, but he was able to demonstrate the sheer breadth of his interests, which included work in pharmacology and hydraulics. He is now primarily recognised for his work in Optics (including his invention of the first telescope and developing the *camera obscura*).

In England the status of the scholar John Dee was not in the least diminished by his interest in the occult, any more than those of his later compatriot, Robert Fludd. Both were astronomers and mathematicians as well as being astrologers and occultists, and their careers, in common with all other of the Renaissance magician-scientists, cannot easily be separated from the rise of genuine science. The separation between the investigation of 'scientific' and 'magical' phenomena was gradual — the distinction was finally made on the basis that the former could convincingly demonstrate its findings, whereas the latter could not. But even such an important figure as Isaac Newton had a life-long interest in Alchemy — certainly he was among the greatest scientist of the modern age, and was probably the last of the 'magicians'.

BRIEF LIST OF PROMINENT MAGICIAN/SCIENTISTS

Filarete (Antonio di Petro Averlino)	1400–1469	Architect, Sculptor (Astrology, Magic)
Giovanni Pico della Miranda	1463–1494	Philosopher
Heinrich Cornelius Agrippa	1486–1535	Magician, Occultist, Astrologer, Alchemist
Paracelsus (Philippus Aureolus Theophrastus Bombastus von Hohenheim)	1493–1541	Physician, Botanist, Alchemist, Occultist, Astrologer
Gerolamo Cardano	1501–1576	Mathematician, Physician, Astrologer, Philosopher, Occultist
John Dee	1527–1608	Mathematician, Astronomer, Astrologer, Occultist
Giambattista della Porta	1535–1615	Mathematician, Philosopher, Alchemist, Astrologer, Occultist
Giordano Bruno	1548–1600	Philosopher, Mathematician, Poet, Astrologer
John Napier	1550–1617	Mathematician, Occultist
Heinrich Khunrath	1560–1605	Philosopher, Physician, Alchemist
Robert Fludd	1574–1637	Mathematician, Cosmologist, Astrologer, Qaballist
Isaac Newton	1643–1727	Physicist, Mathematician, Alchemist, Rosicrucian

DE VRIES, BAROQUE & THE DECLINE OF IMAGINATIVE GEOMETRICISM

By the beginning of the 17th century the fashion for geometric invention was waning. Books on perspective continued to appear in Europe for a very long time to come, and the regular and irregular solids still occasionally featured among the stock illustrations for their theses, but these figures were never again the focus of creative attention. Interest in the 'cosmological' aspects of regular figures also declined. The association with Platonic/Pythagorean concepts had never been entirely forgotten, but were now giving way to a more modern, practical mathematics. From now on there was little, if any, sense of artistic playfulness in connection with regular geometrical figures. This period, of course, saw the emergence of the sumptuous Baroque style, which was firmly associated with the Counter-Reformation and consciously intended to assert the Church's glory and power. Perspective treatises tended now to be produced by Architects involved in this movement, and by mathematicians (particularly by French and Italian Jesuits), who incorporated perspective into the new developments taking place in that discipline

The transition to a grander, more expressive architectural style is epitomised by the drawings of Hans Vredeman de Vries (1527 – 1607), a Dutch architect and engineer. De Vries was responsible for a few modest buildings, and worked on the fortification of Antwerp, but is best known as a theorist. He published a book on garden design in 1583, and another on perspective in 1604, both of which were extremely influential, the latter anticipating the expansive architectural vistas of the Baroque. De Vries does include some geometrical figures in his perspective treatise, but these are very much a prelude to his fantastic architectural visions, both interior and exterior, which were to form the perfect statement for the new 17th century European sense of wealth and power. The principle examples of imaginative geometricism to be found in his work lies in his garden layouts, especially in the garden mazes, of which he seemed particularly fond.

Jacques Androuet Du Cerceau (1549–1584), who came from a distinguished family of architects, was another notable theorist of this period. He produced a volume *Leçons de Perspective Positive*, but here too the primary function of perspective was to provide a dramatic presentation of grand architectural schemes. In this he too was highly successful, to the extent that he is now regarded as 'the inventor of French architecture'. There is, however, very little use of geometrical figures in his treatise.

As mentioned above, the other important direction for perspective studies was mathematical.

ABOVE: A page from de Vries magnificently illustrated, two-Volume book on *Perspective*, published in Amsterdam in 1604.

RIGHT: A page from *Leçons de Perspective Positive* by Jacque Androuet Circeau, another important late-16th century architectural theorist. Circeau's impressive architectural schemes brought him recognition as 'the Father of French Architecture.'

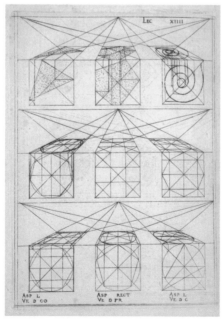

Jean-François Niceron (1613–1646), a French Franciscan monk and mathematician, was an important figure in this movement. He was a pupil of the Jesuit Friar Martin Mersenne, an eminent mathematician who was aware of, and an active defender of the ideas of Galileo, Kepler and Descartes. As well as being a capable mathematician Niceron was an artist of some note, and through these combined interests was drawn into the problems of perspective and other techniques (in particular to their practical applications in religious art). His *La Perspective Curieuse* (Paris, 1638) is essentially an investigation into these subjects. This treatise applies a mathematical approach to anamorphosis (the artful distortion of images) and *trompe l'oeil*, as well as to perspective. He uses regular figures, in a rather conventional treatment of perspective theory, but his book also includes a fine series of stellated bodies. It is interesting too for its demonstration of the ways in which shadows are cast from complex bodies.

Soon after this publication, his compatriot, the Jesuit Father Pierre Le Dubreuil (1602–1670), brought out a huge three-volume tome dealing with perspective, adopting some of Niceron's ideas, and those of various other theorists of the new discipline of Projective Geometry – a project that involved him in a bitter controversy and charges of plagiarism.

ABOVE: Jean-Francois Niceron was a Jesuit mathematician and an artist of some note. He combined these talents in his *La Perspective Curieuse* of 1638.

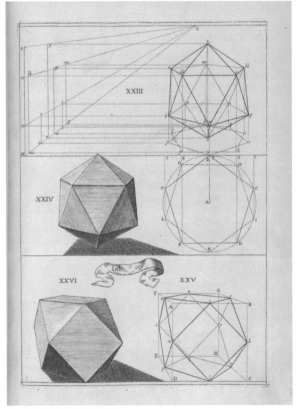

ABOVE: Niceron used polyhedral subjects, of which he shows a fine understanding, to present his theories on perspective.

This work was very popular, however, running to no fewer than twenty editions – but his use of geometrical figures is meagre, limited to a couple of pages of rather plain hollow prisms.

In 1693 one of the more prominent figures of the Baroque period, the Jesuit painter Andrea Pozzo (1642 – 1709), who was particularly famous for his vast *tromp-l'oeil* ceilings, produced a two-volume treatise called *Perspectiva Pictorum et Architectorum*. The goal of this work, as with much of the Baroque movement, was an attempt to restore Catholic artistic hegemony. But it almost marks the end of the association between Geometry in the Euclidean sense and Perspective, since it is entirely concerned with architectural perspective and stage sets and does not include any geometrical figures at all.

The use of geometric figure and diagrams did of course persist; they are found in various later 18th century perspective treatises and are employed to demonstrate perspective principles to this day. But the almost magical linkage between idealistic geometry, the representation of three-dimensions in two, and the puissant cosmological notions of the Classical past were, ironically, all but over by the Age of the Enlightenment.

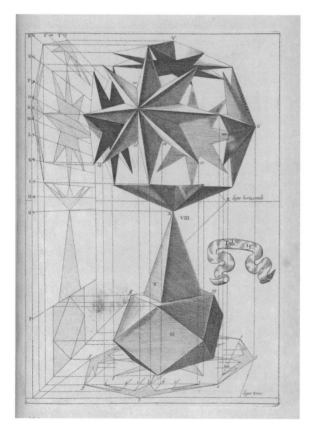

ABOVE: Niceron, who deals with anamorphic and trompe l'oeil techniques in *La Perspective Curieuse*, was particularly skilled in his use of shading to indicate depth.

ABOVE: The third stellation of the dodecahedron, with a fine indication of the perspective of its shadow thrown onto a screen: from *La Perspective Curieuse*.

DE VRIES, BAROQUE & THE DECLINE OF IMAGINATIVE GEOMETRICISM

GEOMETRY & SYMMETRY IN RENAISSANCE GARDEN DESIGN

The Classical/Humanist ideas that were imbibed in the Early Renaissance had, as we have seen, an enormous effect on scholarship, the arts and architecture throughout Western Europe, and it was natural that this influence would also find its expression in garden design. The earliest manifestation of a new, classically-inspired style that used symmetry to express order and beauty naturally occurred in Italy. The earliest proponent of this movement was none other than Leon Battista Alberti, the author of *Della Pittura*, the highly influential book on aesthetics and perspective. For Alberti, beauty consisted in 'the harmony of all parts in relation to one another', in a conscious revival of Classical (and particularly Pythagorean/ Platonic) ideals of number and proportion. His book *De Re Aedifictoria*, published in 1452, was completely sympathetic to the Neoplatonism of the Florentine Academy and promoted its aesthetic ideas to artists, architects and craftsmen – and to garden-makers.

Alberti's Classical-revival theories on garden design, which also derived from the Roman author Vitruvius, were put into effect in the creation of the garden of the Villa Quaracchi around 1495, a scheme that set the fashion for many future formal gardens. Quaracchi had a central axis that ran from the main doorway of the house to the end of the garden. The areas to the left and right were essentially mirror-images, divided by a cross-axis to create regular subdivisions. These areas were further divided into smaller planted plots, or *compartmenti*, some of which had herb hedges in the form of 'knots', layouts that reflected established geometrical patterns which had been used as architectural decoration since the Middle Ages. Tree plantings were in accord with Alberti's instructions and were 'aligned and arranged evenly'. Some of the inspiration for this mode of garden design was drawn from Pliny the Younger's descriptions of his own Tuscan garden-estate in the first century.

The legacy of the Roman world, as it was re-imagined by Renaissance architects and garden builders, laid the template for formal gardens for the next two hundred and fifty years. It was a style that was to be imitated throughout Europe; gardens became grander, ever more symmetrical and perspective conscious. They were used to demonstrate the power and magnificence of their owners, Versailles being the supreme example, but the basic plan, based on supposed Classical precedents, remained the model of formal garden design almost up till the modern period.

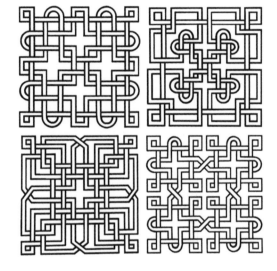

LEFT: Knot designs for Herb Gardens. From Francesco Colonna's *Hypnerotomachia Poliphi*, Venice 1499. Popular throughout the Renaissance it was reprinted as *The Strife of Love* in England in 1592

TOP RIGHT: Maze designs, often from Roman originals, were frequently adopted for Renaissance gardens

BOTTOM: Engravings of geometrical parterres and bosquets from *Traité du Jardinage* by Jacques Boyceau 1638. This was the most important publication of its time to deal with the *Garden à la Française*, the French formal garden.

RIGHT: The original 17th century plans of the gardens of the Chateau of Clagny, near Versailles; designed by Maraine.

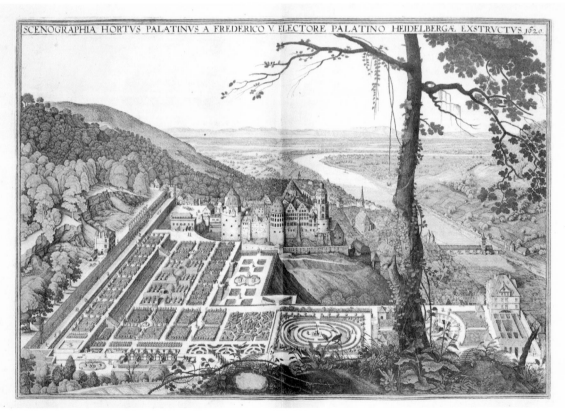

SCENOGRAPHIA HORTVS PALATINVS A FREDERICO V. ELECTORE PALATINO HEIDELBERGÆ EXSTRVCTVS 1620.

ABOVE: The magnificent *Hortus Palatinus*, above the Castle of Heidelberg; painted by Jacques Fourquier in 1618.

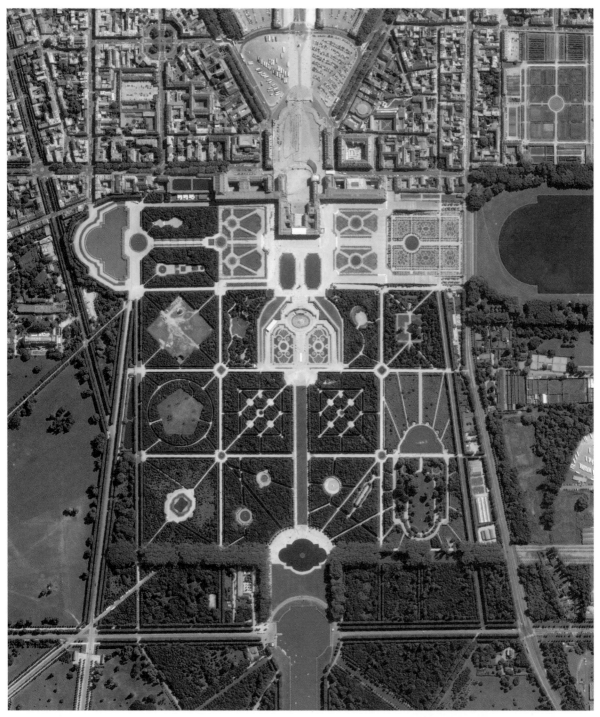

ABOVE: The gardens at Versailles, first commissioned by Louis XIV in 1661, as the absolute epitome of the French formal garden.

GEOMETRY & SYMETRY IN THE RENAISSANCE GARDEN DESIGN   215

THE FORM & STRUCTURE OF CRYSTALS

It is an intriguing coincidence that, just at the time when aesthetic Geometricism was going out of fashion, a scientific interest should arise concerning those most geometric of natural forms, crystals. In the strange way that science sometimes operates, this line of enquiry occurred to various pioneering scientific thinkers at around the same mid-period of the 17ᵗʰ century. The Danish naturalist Nicolas Steno, the Dutch mathematician/physicist Christiaan Huygens, the English polymath Robert Hooke and other great minds of the time addressed this issue; all began to investigate the reason for the external, geometrical form of crystals. Some suspected that this might derive from a regular internal structure of some kind and, interestingly, many made the connection between the delicate forms of snow-flakes and the regularities of mineral crystals. Knowingly or not, they were of course following a trail initiated by the avowed Platonist Johannes Kepler in his 1611 essay *Strena seu de Nive Sexangula* (on the 'Six-cornered Snowflake'; see pg. 182). Kepler did not pursue his investigations into regular geometrical structures in Nature, but by 1669 Steno was able to publish his Law of constant angles, which became the basis of morphological crystallography.*

In the course of his study of Light Christiaan Huygens also became intrigued by crystalline regularities. He came to the same intuited notion as Kepler, that these features arose 'from the arrangement of small, equal and invisible particles'. Robert Hooke is justifiably famous for his *Micrographia* which, in 1665, presented an awed London public with intricately detailed pictures of microscopic subjects, among which were depictions of fleas and lice blown up to monstrous proportions. But Hooke also examined the crystalline structure of snowflakes under his microscope, and went much further than Kepler in explaining how close-packing arrangements of spheres might account for the various habits of crystals.

Brilliant as they were however, none of these insights were followed by further sustained investigation. Most of these thinkers had many other interests, moreover, the field of crystallography was hampered by the lack of quantitative techniques, i.e. the means of accurately determining hardness, angularity etc. – and the absence of any convincing atomic/molecular theory was another constraining factor. The slow progress in crystallographic studies was to radically change in the following century

---

* The law that he introduced in *De Solido intra Solidum Natualiter Contendo* states that the angles between corresponding faces on crystals of the same mineral were constant. Streno does in fact refer to Kepler's *Strena* in this work.

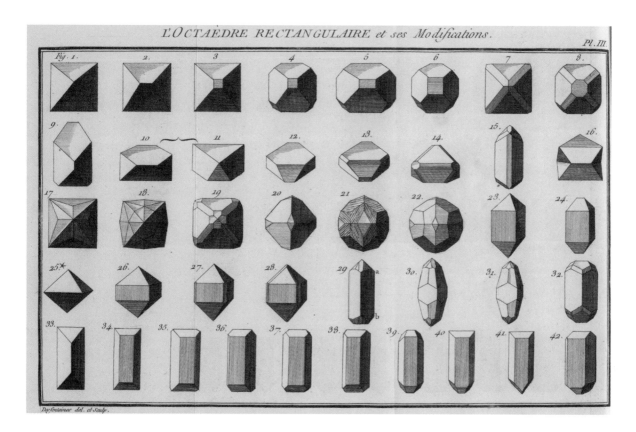

however, with the work of two remarkable French scientists.

In 1783 a self-taught ex-army officer, Romé de l'Isle, published the massive, four-volume set of his *Cristallographie*, the summation of some twenty years of mineral and crystalline research. During this time, De l'Isle had rediscovered Steno's Law of Constant Angles and had used a *goniometer* (a device, invented by one of his assistants, Arnould Carangeot), to classify 450 distinct crystal types. To encourage sales of his lavish book De l'Isle made ceramic models of each of these forms to accompany the volumes. There were 448 of these, made in the Royal Porcelain Factory at Sèvres. Unsurprisingly, *Cristallographie* and its crystal models proved to be a great success, selling to Museums and Educational establishments throughout Europe. These days they are antiquarian objects of great value.

ABOVE: A page from Romé de l'Isles *Cristallographie* of 1783, depicting Octahedral/Rectangular crystalline variants.

Unfortunately, De l'Isle had been patronised by aristocrats and, like them, became a victim of history. The Revolution, which saw the establishment of the Republic in 1792, meant that he was no longer *persona grata* on the French scientific scene. His place and interests were, however, taken over by an equally energetic individual, a priest named René Just Haüy. Haüy, who had the advantage of being favoured by the new Bonapartiste regime, brought a new sense of order to the accumulation of data on crystal morphologies with his theories of Rational Indices. He postulated that crystalline structure was based on *molecules soustractive*, a progressive series of polyhedral building blocks, and demonstrated that these, by addition and subtraction of rows, could form cubes, rhombohedra and other typical crystal shapes. Haüy had no real conception of the scale of molecules proper, of the billions of atoms involved in even the smallest of crystalline formations, but his ideas, though later superseded, presented a rational basis for the variety of crystal types and he is rightly regarded as the founder of the science of Crystallography.

Crystal models continued to be made as aids to teaching crystallography long after Romé de l'isle and Haüy's collections had become outdated. In fact they still are used by those who want their students to get a firm, material understanding of the subject, but the advent of X-ray crystallography in the early 20th century, and the more recent techniques of computer modelling, have made them seem somewhat old-fashioned. Perhaps surprisingly though there is still sufficient demand to sustain at least one supplier, the family-run Krantz company, which, remarkably, has been making its models since 1837.

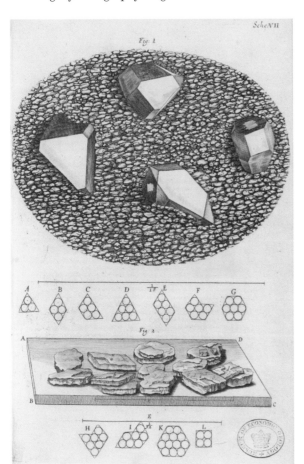

ABOVE: Robert Hooke's crystal studies from his *Micrographia*, 1665.

ABOVE: Wooden models of crystal forms by de l'Isle and Haüy.

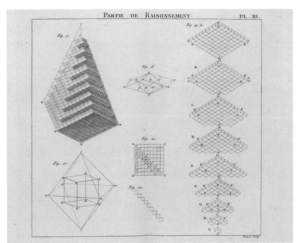

ABOVE: Haüy's arrangements of *molecules soustractives* demonstrating his Law of Decrement; from his *Traité de Cristallographie*, 1832.

IN CONCLUSION

With Morphological Crystallography there is a sense in which we come full circle in this investigation. It is very likely that the seminal theories of the Pythagoreans regarding geometrical forms were partially inspired by natural crystalline formations. They would certainly have been have been aware and intrigued by such objects. Among other crystals that occurred in their part of the world were those of iron pyrites, which appear in both cubic and dodecahedral habits. In fact, the precise symmetries of crystal forms must always have intrigued humans. Their purity of form stands in complete contrast with the chaotic complexity of much of the rest of nature, and it is hardly surprising that they would have attracted magical connotations, just as they later became the focus of scientific speculation.

The purity of geometry makes it an inspirational subject. For the Pythagoreans, and later for Plato, it had undertones of the religious – and through their contribution to Western thought it has retained this association of otherworldliness. Geometry is deeply interwoven into Western culture. In mathematics, after a decline in the first part of the 20th century, interest in Geometry has well and truly revived largely through the efforts of Donald Coxeter. Beloved by all those interested in regular polytopes,

ABOVE: Donald Coxeter, Anglo-Canadian mathematician (1907–2003) 'The Man who saved Geometry'.

he showed how Geometry is at the very core of all mathematics, championed the subject when it seemed to be going out of fashion, and was always fully aware of its aesthetic as well as its mathematical value.

And, in quite different ways, there are many artists throughout the world who are making fresh interpretations of this old subject. This is all as it should be. After all, geometric figures in two, three or more dimensions are merely points and lines – what could be more elemental, or more abstract, or inspiring?

GEOMETRICAL/PERSPECTIVE TREATISES OF THE c15TH–17TH

And other relevant publications, arranged by date of publication

De Prospectiva pigendi, *c.*1470; Piero della Francesca (*c.*1410–492)

Libellus de Quinque Corporibus Regularibus, *c.*1480; Piero della Francesca (*c.*1410–1492)

Euclid's ' Elementa Geometriae, Venice,1482; Erhard Ratdolt (1442–1528)

De Divina Proportione, Venice, 1509; Luca Pacioli (1446–1517); illustrated by Leonardo Da Vinci (1452–1519)

Underweysung der Messung mit dem Zirckel und Richscheyt, Nuremberg, 1525; Albrecht Durer (1471–1528)

Vier Bucher von Menschlicher Proportion, Nuremberg, 1528; Albrecht Durer (1471–1528)

Ein schon nutzlich Buchlein, Nuremberg, 1531; Hieronymus Rodler (*d.*1539)

Ein aigentliche und grundliche anweysung in die Geometria, Nuremberg, 1543; Augustin Hirschvogel (1503–1553)

Geometrische und Perspektivische Zeichnungen, Nuremberg?, c.1560; Anonymous (*c.*1565–1600)

Livres de Perspective, Paris, 1560; Jean Cousin (1490–1560)

Des Circles und Richtscheyts, Nuremberg, 1564; Heinrich Lautensack (1520–1568)

Geometria et Perspectiva, Augsberg, 1567; Lorenz Stoer (*c.*1540–1620)

Perspectiva Literaria, Nuremberg, 1567, 1596; Johannes Lencker (1551?-1585)

Perspectiva Corporum Regularium, Nuremberg, 1568; Wentzel Jamnitzer (1508–1585)

La Pratica della Perspettiva, Venice, 1569; Daniel Barbaro (1513–1570)

Perspectiva, Nuremberg, 1571; Johannes Lencker (1551?–1585)

Lecons de Perspective Positive, Paris, 1576; Jaques Androuet Du Cerceau (1549–1584)

Mysterium Cosmographicum, Tubingen, 1596; 1621; Johannes Kepler (1571–1630)

La Practica di Prospettiva, Venice, 1596; Lorenzo Sirigatti, *d.*1625

Extract der Geometriae und Perspectivae, Nuremberg, 1598; Paul Pfinzing (1554–1599)

Perspective, Amsterdam, 1604; Jan Vredeman de Vries (1527–*c.*1607)

Strena seu de Niva Sexangula, Frankfurt, 1611: Johannes Kepler (1571–1630)

Praxis Perspective, Leipzig, 1615; Lucas Brunn (1572–1628)

Harmonices Mundi, Frankfurt, 1619: Johannes Kepler (1571–1630)

Prospettiva Pratica, Florence, 1625; Pietro Accolti (1579–1642)

Perspectivische Reiss Kunst, Augsburg, 1625, Peter Halt (uncertain)

La Perspective Curieuse, Paris, 1638; Jean-Francois Niceron (1613–1646)

La Perspective Pratique, Paris, 1642; Pierre Le Dubreuil (1602–1670)

Aerarium Philosophiaae Mathematicae, Rome, 1648; Mario Bettini (1582–1657)

Perspectiva pictorum et Architectoerum, Augsburg, 1693; Andrea Pozzo (1642–1709)

Linear Perspective, London, 1715; Brook Taylor (1685–1731)

Lucidum Prospectivae Speculum, Augsburg, 1727; Paul Heinecken (1680–1746)

REFERENCES / FURTHER READING

Anderson, Kirsti: ' *The Geometry of an Art: the history of the mathematical theory of perspective ...* '; Springer, N.Y. 2007.

Bedini, Silvio: *'The Perspective Machine of Wentzel Jamnitzer';* Technology and Culture, April, 1968, Volume 9, Number 2.

Cromwell, Peter R: *Polyhedra;* Cambridge University Press, 1997, 2004.

Gluch, Sibylle: *The Craft's use of Geometry in 16ᵗʰc. Germany;* University of Dresden, 2007.

Hart, George W: *Polyhedra and Art through History,* www.georgehart.com

Kemp, Martin: *The Science of Art: Optical themes in western art;* Yale University Press, 1990.

Pfaff, Dorothea: *Lorenz Stoer: Geometria et Perspectiva;* LMU Publikatione, http.//epub.ub.uni-muenchen.de.

Richter, Fleur: *Die Àsthetik geometrischer Körper in der Renaissance;* Verlag Gerd Hatje, 1995.

Smith, Jeffry Chipps: *Nuremberg and the Topologies of Expectation;* Journal of the Northern Renaissance, Spring, 2009.

Schreiber, P: *A New Hypothesis on Durer's Enigmatic Polyhedron in His Copper Engraving 'Melencolia';* Historia Math. 26. 369–377, 1999.

Sutton, Daud: *Platonic & Archimedean Solids;* Walker & Company, 2002.

Van den Broeke, Albert and Ruttkay, Zsofia: *A Closer Look at Jamnitzer's Polyhedra';* University of Twente.

Veltman, Kim H: *'Geometric Games. A History of the Not so Regular Solids'* 1990. *The sources and Literature of Perspective,* www.sumscorp.com

Wood, Christopher S.: *The Perspective Treatise in Ruins:* Studies in the History of Art, Symposium Papers XXXVI, Washington Nat. Gall. Of Art, CASVA, 2003 (Republished with CD-ROM edition of Lorenz Stoer: *'Geometria et Perpectiva'* Harald Fischer Verlag, Erlangen, 2006).

INDEX

PICTURE CREDITS